Your
English
Springer Spaniel

By Reed F. Hankwitz

Compiled and Edited by

William W. Denlinger and R. Annabel Rathman

DENLINGER'S

Fairfax, Virginia 22030

Dedication

To my wife, Trude, for without her help, I would have been unable to enjoy my activities in the dog world the past twenty-five years.

Copyright © 1973

By William W. Denlinger, Fairfax, Virginia 22030.

All rights reserved, including the right to reproduce this book, or portions thereof, in any form, except for the inclusion of brief quotations in a review. This book was completely manufactured in the United States of America and published simultaneously in Canada by General Publishing Company, Toronto, Canada.

International Standard Book Number: 0-87714-007-3

Library of Congress Catalog Card Number: 72-80629

The Author, Reed F. Hankwitz, awarding Best of Breed to Ch. Kenlor Animation at the Santa Ana Kennel Club Show, September 1966.

Foreword

Going back over twenty years of living, talking, raising, judging, and dreaming Springers, I have often wondered how I would write a book to help a newcomer in the breed and to lighten his load when it came to starting in dogs.

There are so many simple things which can be done to get the proper start and which will enable one to start enjoying a dog much sooner.

There have been some fine books written on the breed and they have made things much easier for all concerned, but how many look to the future? Most of the information I got from them was either general or past history, leaving several gaps in between—going back with nothing going ahead. Pedigrees either covered a lot of unknowns when I was new in the breed, or jumped over them.

The interest of the average dog fancier is said to continue for about five years. The turnover is tremendous, but every year registration of purebred dogs is on the increase, and that is encouraging, especially since Springers show a gradual and steady increase.

Today, we have many more prefixes than we had twenty-five years ago. Many of the older ones are gone but many more are to come in the future. The sooner you know the prefixes and recognize them, the easier it will be for you to figure out what you want to do, and how to do it right. There is a difference between breeding just to get pups and breeding for good ones. The dogs can do the one, but you must do both—and then it's up to the judges to go on from there.

Be sure you get all the information that is available, and don't just read about Springers. Read and then ask and read again if you are new in the dog game, but get the information first. That is what this book is intended to be about: to help a novice owner to get the most and the best for his Springer.

It is the author's hope that you will get a good start toward acquiring enough ideas to carry you on far into the future and to take your place among the greats. It will, at least, help you to get on your way. And I am sure you will get lots of help from others in the fancy if you ask sensible questions and follow through in a sensible way.

Luck——

R. F. HANKWITZ

Contents

Selecting the Springer Spaniel Puppy 7
The Adult Springer 13
Grooming the Springer 29
Grooming and General Coat Care 33
Nutrition 39
Maintaining the Dog's Health 45
Housing Your Dog 53
History of the Genus *Canis* 57
History of the English Springer Spaniel 65
Pillars of the Breed—1920 to 1970 73
Top Kennels in the United States 83
Manners for the Family Dog 97
Bench Shows 105
Obedience Competition 111
Genetics 117
Breeding and Whelping 123
Personality of the Springer 129
The Springer in the Obedience Ring 135
The Springer in the Field 141
Training the Gun Dog 147
Retrieving 155

Judy and her puppies, by Oak, whelped April 2, 1938

Selecting the Springer Spaniel Puppy

Today, through the media, people are told how to feed dogs, how to train them, how to show them, and how and where to buy them. Despite this accumulation of advice, it can be a lot safer to contact someone who owns a dog of the breed you want—someone who knows an honest breeder with extensive knowledge of the breed. When dealing with a breeder, there is no waiting for papers and no question of the dog's authenticity. And there is no question as to the quality of the dam and sire, for the purchaser normally can see one or both.

Springer puppies are cute, and, if healthy, look much alike the first two months, so their actual quality often mystifies a novice. After the first Springer has lived in his home, an owner usually knows a lot more about what he wants to get when it comes to purchasing a puppy. He has made a study of the breed, he has studied the Standard—or at least has read it—he has compared his dog with others, and perhaps he has gone to a show—either point or match—and possibly a field trial.

Perhaps when our novice goes to look for a Springer, he is unable to find a dog to match his expectations. He may find dogs with head pieces too long or too short, too much or too little bone, too much or too little coat, a long back or a short back, long legs or short legs, and feet going east and west. Then, after being just about ready to give up and buy a pony or let his daughter have a cat, he starts talking over lunch to a friend who can speak of nothing except the Springer he has just purchased. The friend quotes the Standard and the breeder and drops names of famous dogs in his Springer's pedigree. Slowly our novice picks up new enthusiasm and decides to go and see this paragon.

He drives over, and, well—let's just say his friend made a good deal. He bought a well-bred puppy from an honest breeder who did a conscientious job of breeding, then sold the dogs after evaluating them as to their quality as pets or show or field stock, and priced them accordingly. The friend bought a Springer to show in the conformation ring, and so far as can be determined at this point, got a show puppy: one with a good head, fine blaze, chiseled face, good square muzzle, clear eyes, well-set ears, good leather, a good clean neck which looks adequate, good brisket and nice rib cage, a square rear and a

good tail set, a Springer up on its pads with straight front of proper width—and with no evidence that any of these qualities will be different later.

Well, if the novice is you, do your homework, and do not hurry. Make up your mind as to the type of dog you want—whether for the field, for show, or as a pet. If you want a pet, buy it, but don't expect a breeder to sell you a show prospect if you tell him you want a pet.

Study the Standard until it becomes a blueprint of specifications for a Springer and is indelibly stamped on your brain. A conscientious breeder will help you assess the quality of the puppies in the litter, but shop around and compare. Get someone who knows dogs to go with you and help you analyze the qualities of the puppies you see. Then make your selection on the basis of all those you have seen and get the puppy that you feel will most nearly fulfill your desires.

Avoid the puppy that exhibits any traces of shyness. Make sure the one you select doesn't prefer to be by itself in the far corner of the puppy pen—that it doesn't duck when a food dish is dropped nearby. Look for the one that dashes at you, licks your fingers up to your wrist watch, makes friends first, and then tours the environs to check on sundry matters—the one that is first out to greet strangers and last to be put back in the pen.

Check the teeth for the correct bite. Get a good feel of the ribs and loin. Watch the puppies walk—or run, if they are old enough. Examine the gait. There will be some puppyishness about it, but even at an early age it can show the smoothness which you will want later.

Above all, make sure that the dog you select is a typical Springer. Remember, it costs as much to feed a mediocre dog as it does to feed a good one, and nothing deflates a dog owner's ego more than to have someone say, "Oh, you have a dog now," instead of, "What an adorable Springer pup!"

"Hello! to you from us!"

Pup and moccasin

After you have asked all possible questions of the breeder, then take luck by the hand, and remember it's a gamble because many things can happen before the puppy matures, as breeders, owners, and exhibitors of the top ones and the "never were" can tell you.

When it comes to the final choice, you will be on your own. Your decision will govern the quality of the dog you select. What you have learned will be the factor that dominates your choice, and if you pray a little hopefully, the puppy will develop into a fine dog. When you purchase a Springer, you get odds that he will.

By the time your puppy is eight weeks old he will profile a picture that begins to show what he'll be like when he matures. Many breeders feel this is the time to evaluate all puppies, for it is the time when Springers really shape up. Had you been considering two or three that looked on a par a few weeks earlier, you would now note a marked difference between them. You wouldn't need to refer to the Standard, for your eye would detect the difference. Just don't become too knowledgeable or too critical an authority. No dog has ever been whelped perfect, anymore than any human being has ever been born perfect, and changes will keep coming along as the dog progresses toward maturity. This is a grand time of life, as the puppy grows bone and muscle first, then blooms all over. And the dogs often look like the bitches, and the bitches often act like growing girls—but all look more like Springers every day.

Make your vet your confidant. Ask his advice on how to condition your dog and how to help him develop and mature properly. Whether you intend to show your dog or not, every bit of advice and help your vet gives you will pay dividends.

Make certain that your vet gets stool samples regularly, puts your dog on a regular worming schedule, and gives him his shots—advancing him from puppy shots to permanent ones. If your Springer is a

A nestful—Jeannie and pups.

Jeannie's pups eating.

Pups in basket.

male, see that your vet checks for monorchidism and cryptorchidism, for these conditions are sometimes hard to ascertain in young puppies. Monorchidism (the lack of one testicle) and cryptorchidism (the lack of both) are heritable traits, so a monorchid should not be used for breeding, even though he is capable of producing puppies. A cryptorchid cannot, of course, produce offspring. Monorchidism and cryptorchidism are grounds for disqualification in the show ring. This is an American Kennel Club rule and applies to all breeds.

As your dog (and, incidentally, when I say "dog" I mean Springer —dog or bitch) gets older, it will be a very good thing to have your vet prepare an X-ray and the papers needed for a hip dysplasia checkup. Hip dysplasia is a defect that is still something of a mystery, but may be due to an inherited, recessive factor. Consequently, animals known to possess it should not be used for breeding. The condition consists of an insufficient or incorrect formation of the hip socket bone, so that the head of the bone which forms the joint is not correctly seated and retained. It appears to be especially prevalent in animals that are allowed to become too heavy in puppyhood. Many authorities feel that in addition to hereditary factors, responsibility for the condition may lie in part in environmental factors such as overfeeding. Conscientious breeders have their breeding animals checked by X-ray, which is the best method for determining whether they are free of the affliction. Puppies are often offered with a guarantee against hip dysplasia, which is a most desirable provision. So have your dog certified, not just to protect him and to protect yourself, but to protect the future of the breed as well.

By the time the puppy is wormed, has had shots and X-rays, plus a physical examination with more strange noises and smells, the poor little tyke may have no difficulty forgetting that familiar whelping box, his litter mates, his warm mother, and the coziness of it all. But remember, it usually takes time and effort on the part of the new owner if the puppy is to adjust. And it helps a great deal to talk to him, to fondle him, and to keep him close to the family circle.

Be sure to mail that registration slip to The American Kennel Club —with your dog's name and your name on it—so he can be given his permanent registration number and take his place in American dogdom.

With your dog registered with The American Kennel Club, he— and you, as well—will be ready to sally forth in quest of glory. Once you are the owner of a Springer, life begins.

Veterans Class at Eastern English Springer Spaniel Club Specialty Show, Ridgefield, Connecticut.

Eastern English Springer Spaniel Club Specialty Show.

The Adult Springer

The Standard for the English Springer Spaniel was adopted in 1956 by the English Springer Spaniel Field Trial Association, parent club of the breed, and approved by The American Kennel Club. It provides a description of the specifications of the ideal Springer to aid in breeding, selecting, and evaluating puppies, and to show breeders, owners, judges, and others what to look for in an adult English Springer Spaniel. The Standard is as follows:

STANDARD OF THE ENGLISH SPRINGER SPANIEL
(Approved June 12, 1956)

General Appearance and Type—The English Springer Spaniel is a medium-size sporting dog with a neat, compact body, and a docked tail. His coat is moderately long, glossy, usually liver and white or black and white, with feathering on his legs, ears, chest and brisket. His pendulous ears, soft gentle expression, sturdy build and friendly wagging tail proclaim him unmistakably a member of the ancient family of spaniels. He is above all a well proportioned dog, free from exaggeration, nicely balanced in every part. His carriage is proud and upstanding, body deep, legs strong and muscular with enough length to carry him with ease. His short level back, well developed thighs, good shoulders, excellent feet, suggest power, endurance, agility. Taken as a whole he looks the part of a dog that can go and keep going under difficult hunting conditions, and moreover he enjoys what he is doing. At his best he is endowed with style, symmetry, balance, enthusiasm and is every inch a sporting dog of distinct spaniel character, combining beauty and utility. To be penalized: Those lacking true English Springer type in conformation, expression, or behavior.

Temperament—The typical Springer is friendly, eager to please, quick to learn, willing to obey. In the show ring he should exhibit poise, attentiveness, tractability, and should permit himself to be examined by the judge without resentment or cringing. To be penalized: Excessive timidity, with due allowance for puppies and novice exhibits. But no dog to receive a ribbon if he behaves in vicious manner toward handler or judge. Aggressiveness toward other dogs in the ring *not* to be construed as viciousness.

Size and Proportion—The Springer is built to cover rough ground with agility and reasonable speed. He should be kept to medium size—neither too small nor too large and heavy to do the work for which he is intended. The ideal shoulder height for dogs is 20 inches; for bitches, 19 inches. Length of topline (the distance from the top of the shoulders to the root of the tail) should be approximately equal to the dog's shoulder height—never longer than his height —and not appreciably less. The dog too long in body, especially when long in loin, tires easily and lacks the compact outline characteristic of the breed. Equally undesirable is the dog too short in body for the length of his legs, a condition that destroys his balance and restricts the gait.

Ch. Beryltown Fiery Prince, C.D.

Ch. Beryltown Lucky Christmas.

Ch. Beryltown Red-Hot Rocket.

Weight is dependent on the dog's other dimensions: a 20-inch dog, well proportioned, in good condition should weight about 49-55 pounds. The resulting appearance is a well-knit, sturdy dog with good but not too heavy bone, in no way coarse or ponderous. To be penalized: Over-heavy specimens, cloddy in build. Leggy individuals, too tall for their length and substance. Oversize or undersize specimens (those more than one inch under or over the breed ideal).

Color and Coat—Color may be liver or black with white markings; liver and white (or black and white) with tan markings; blue or liver roan; or predominantly white with tan, black or liver markings. On ears, chest, legs and belly the Springer is nicely furnished with a fringe of feathering (of moderate heaviness). On his head, front or forelegs, and below hocks on front of hind legs the hair is short and fine. The body coat is flat or wavy, of medium length, sufficiently dense to be water-proof, weather-proof and thorn-proof. The texture fine and the hair should have the clean, glossy, live appearance indicative of good health. It is legitimate to trim about head, feet, ears; to remove dead hair; to thin and shorten excess feathering particularly from the hocks to the feet and elsewhere as required to give a smart, clean appearance. To be penalized: Rough, curly coat. Over-trimming especially of the body coat. Any chopped, barbered or artificial effect. Excessive feathering that destroys the clean outline desirable in a sporting dog. Off colors such as lemon, red or orange not to place.

Head—The head is impressive without being heavy. Its beauty lies in a combination of strength and refinement. It is important that the size and proportion be in balance with the rest of the dog. Viewed in profile the head should appear approximately the same length as the neck and should blend with the body in substance. The skull (upper head) to be of medium length, fairly broad, flat on top, slightly rounded at the sides and back. The occiput bone inconspicuous, rounded rather than peaked or angular. The foreface (head in front of the eyes) approximately the same length as the skull, and in harmony as to width and general character. Looking down on the head the muzzle to appear to be about one half the width of the skull. As the skull rises from the foreface it makes a brow or "stop," divided by a groove or fluting between the eyes. This groove continues upward and gradually disappears as it reaches the middle of the forehead. The amount of "stop" can best be described as moderate. It must not be a pronounced feature as in the Clumber Spaniel. Rather it is a subtle rise where the muzzle blends into the upper head, further emphasized by the groove and by the position and shape of the eyebrows which should be well-developed. The stop, eyebrow and the chiseling of the bony structure around the eye sockets contribute to the Springer's beautiful and characteristic expression.

Viewed in profile the topline of the skull and the muzzle lie in two approximately parallel planes. The nasal bone should be straight, with no inclination downward toward the tip of the nose which gives a down-faced look so undesirable in this breed. Neither should the nasal bone be concave resulting in a "dish-faced" profile; nor convex giving the dog a Roman nose. The jaws to be of sufficient length to allow the dog to carry game easily; fairly square, lean, strong, and even (neither undershot nor overshot). The upper lip to come down full and rather square to cover the line of the lower jaw, but lips not to be pendulous nor exaggerated. The nostrils, well opened and broad, liver color or black depending on the color of the coat. Flesh-colored ("Dudley noses") or spotted ("butterfly noses") are undesirable. The cheeks to be flat (not rounded, full or thick) with nice chiseling under the eyes. To be penalized: Oval, pointed or heavy skull. Cheeks prominently rounded, thick and protruding. Too much or too little stop. Over heavy muzzle. Muzzle too short, too thin, too nar-

row. Pendulous slobbery lips. Under- or over-shot jaws—a very serious fault, to be heavily penalized. *Teeth*—The teeth should be strong, clean, not too small; and when the mouth is closed the teeth should meet in an even bite or a close scissors bite (the lower incisors touching the inside of the upper incisors). To be penalized: Any deviation from above description. One or two teeth slightly out of line not to be considered a serious fault, but irregularities due to faulty jaw formation to be severely penalized.

Eyes—More than any other feature the eyes contribute to the Springer's appeal. Color, placement, size influence expression and attractiveness. The eyes to be of medium size, neither small, round, full and prominent, nor bold and hard in expression. Set rather well apart and fairly deep in their sockets. The color of the iris to harmonize with the color of the coat, preferably a good dark hazel in the liver dogs and black or deep brown in the black and white specimens. The expression to be alert, kindly, trusting. The lids, tight with little or no haw showing. To be penalized: Eyes yellow or brassy in color or noticeably lighter than the coat. Sharp expression indicating unfriendly or suspicious nature. Loose droopy lids. Prominent haw (the third eyelid or membrane in the inside corner of the eye).

Ears—The correct ear-set is on a level with the line of the eye; on the side of skull and not too far back. The flaps to be long and fairly wide, hanging close to the cheeks, with no tendency to stand up or out. The leather, thin, approximately long enough to reach the tip of the nose. To be penalized: Short round ears. Ears set too high or too low or too far back on the head.

Neck—The neck to be moderately long, muscular, slightly arched at the crest gradually blending into sloping shoulders. Not noticeably upright nor coming into the body at an abrupt angle. To be penalized: Short neck, often the sequence to steep shoulders. Concave neck, sometimes called ewe neck or upside down neck (the opposite of arched). Excessive throatiness.

Body—The body to be well coupled, strong, compact; the chest deep but not so wide or round as to interfere with the action of the front legs; the brisket sufficiently developed to reach to the level of the elbows. The ribs fairly long, springing gradually to the middle of the body then tapering as they approach the end of the ribbed section. The back (section between the withers and loin) to be straight and strong, with no tendency to dip or roach. The loins

Ch. Chinoe's
Adamant James

to be strong, short; a slight arch over loins and hip bones. Hips nicely rounded, blending smoothly into hind legs. The resulting topline slopes *very gently* from withers to tail—the line from withers to back descending without a sharp drop; the back practically level; arch over hips somewhat lower than the withers; croup sloping gently to base of tail; tail carried to follow the natural line of the body. The bottom line, starting on a level with the elbows, to continue backwards with almost no up-curve until reaching the end of the ribbed section, then a more noticeable up-curve to the flank, but not enough to make the dog appear small waisted or "tucked up." To be penalized: Body too shallow, indicating lack of brisket. Ribs too flat, sometimes due to immaturity. Ribs too round (barrel-shaped), hampering the gait. Swayback (dip in back), indicating weakness or lack of muscular development, particularly to be seen when dog is in action and viewed from the side. Roach back (too much arch over loin and extending forward into middle section). Croup falling away too sharply; or croup too high—unsightly faults, detrimental to outline and good movement. Topline sloping sharply, indicating steep withers (straight shoulder placement) and a too low tail-set.

Tail—The Springer's tail is an index both to his temperament and his conformation. Merry tail action is characteristic. The proper set is somewhat low following the natural line of the croup. The carriage should be nearly horizontal, slightly elevated when dog is excited. Carried straight up is untypical of the breed. The tail should not be docked too short and should be well fringed with wavy feather. It is legitimate to shape and shorten the feathering but enough should be left to blend with the dog's other furnishings. To be penalized: Tail habitually upright. Tail set too high or too low. Clamped down tail (indicating timidity or undependable temperament, even less to be desired than the tail carried too gaily).

Forequarters—Efficient movement in front calls for proper shoulders. The blades sloping back to form an angle with the forearm of approximately 90 degrees which permits the dog to swing his forelegs forward in an easy manner. Shoulders (fairly close together at the tips) to lie flat and mold smoothly into the contour of the body. The forelegs to be straight with the same degree of size to the foot. The bone, strong, slightly flattened, not too heavy or round. The knee, straight, almost flat; the pasterns short, strong; elbows close to the body with free action from the shoulders. To be penalized: Shoulders set at a steep angle limiting the stride. Loaded shoulders (the blades standing out from the body by overdevelopment of the muscles). Loose elbows, crooked legs. Bone too light or too coarse and heavy. Weak pasterns that let down the feet at a pronounced angle.

Hindquarters—The Springer should be shown in hard muscular condition, well developed in hips and thighs and the whole rear assembly should suggest strength and driving power. The hip joints to be set rather wide apart and the hips nicely rounded. The thighs broad and muscular; the stifle joint strong and moderately bent. The hock joint somewhat rounded, not small and sharp in contour, and moderately angulated. Leg from hock joint to foot pad, short and strong with good bone structure. When viewed from the rear the hocks to be parallel whether the dog is standing or in motion. To be penalized: Too little or too much angulation. Narrow, undeveloped thighs. Hocks too short or too long (a proportion of ⅓ the distance from hip joint to foot is ideal). Flabby muscles. Weakness of joints.

Feet—The feet to be round, or slightly oval, compact, well arched, medium size with thick pads, well feathered between the toes. Excess hair to be removed to show the natural shape and size of the foot. To be penalized: Thin, open or splayed feet (flat with spreading toes). Hare foot (long, rather narrow foot).

Movement—In judging the Springer there should be emphasis on proper movement which is the final test of a dog's conformation and soundness. Prerequisite to good movement is balance of the front and rear assemblies. The two must match in angulation and muscular development if the gait is to be smooth and effortless. Good shoulders laid back at an angle that permits a long stride are just as essential as the excellent rear quarters that provide the driving power. When viewed from the front the dog's legs should appear to swing forward in a free and easy manner, with no tendency for the feet to cross over or interfere with each other. Viewed from the rear the hocks should drive well under the body following on a line with the forelegs, the rear legs parallel, neither too widely nor too closely spaced. Seen from the side the Springer should exhibit a good, long forward stride, without high-stepping or wasted motion. To be penalized: Short choppy stride, mincing steps with up and down movement, hopping. Moving with forefeet wide, giving roll or swing to body. Weaving or crossing of fore or hind feet. Cowhocks—hocks turning in toward each other.

In judging the English Springer Spaniel the over-all picture is a primary consideration. It is urged that the judge look for type which includes general appearance, outline and temperament and also for soundness especially as seen when the dog is in motion. Inasmuch as the dog with a smooth easy gait must be reasonably sound and well balanced he is to be highly regarded in the show ring, however, not to the extent of forgiving him for not looking like an English Springer Spaniel. A quite untypical dog, leggy, foreign in head and expression, may move well. But he should not be placed over a good all-round specimen that has a minor fault in movement. It should be remembered that the English Springer Spaniel is first and foremost a sporting dog of the spaniel family and he must look and behave and move in character.

Ch. Felicia's Fair Lady, going Best of Winners at 1968 Worcester Show. Judge, Reed F. Hankwitz.

Ch. Schwedekrest Lo and Behold

"General Appearance and Type" is an appropriate heading for the first section of the Standard, for in a breed where dogs serve as pets, for show, and in the field, we often find the dogs in each category most similar, yet each category different from others in the breed.

For instance, pet dogs are sometimes bred without the same acumen or thought used in breeding dogs in the other two categories. Also, Springers, being Spaniels, are by inclination ready to eat anything, anytime, anywhere. The result is that they often get a bit "blimpy" late in life—as they sleep more, rest more, and emulate their human owners more in being inclined to be less active physically as they take it easy.

Show dogs are closer to the Standard than the other types. The Standard was written and agreed upon only by members of the parent club, which started as a field trial club, although most dogs in the field miss the breed Standard considerably. This is true of many Sporting breeds and is also true in England, where owners show dogs and hunt over dogs, but where they have slowly, over the years, actually developed two types of dogs in the same breed. Beauty is in the eyes of the beholder—and each type Springer is bred to be the most beautiful for use in its class. American Champion, Canadian Dual Cham-

Ch. Daphne of Recess

Ch. Caroleigh Brown Blazer.

Ch. Beryltown Lively Rocket, C.D.

Can. and Am. Ch. Sandhurst Robin Hood.

Ch. Huval's Cinderella

Ch. Beryltown Lively Empress, C.D.

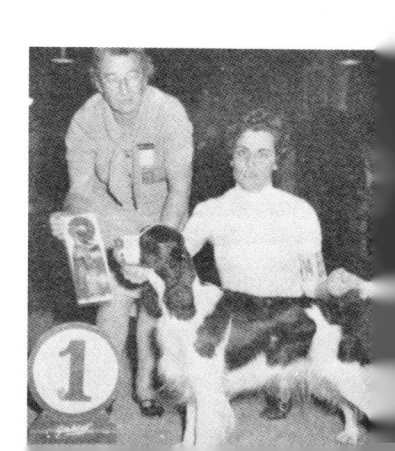

Ch. Ring-A-Ding's Sir Lancelot.

Ch. Hunting Ridge Tamarack, Ch. Tamridge Twinkling Star, Ch. Tamridge Talisman, and Tamridge High Noon.

pion Dan Dee of Melilotus, who acquired his title in 1959, was a show-type dog—taking a class in a National Specialty and also in the Field Dog Class. He was not a dual champion at the time of the Specialty and created quite a bit of amusement among the professional field trial handlers when he was shown in the Field Dog Class—but he did have his Canadian certificate and finished a month or so after the Specialty as a dual champion in Canada.

But the point is that a Standard must cover a breed in its entirety and be set up so that it definitely describes the most typical members of the breed. In the case of Springers, many are pet and show dogs—and most are predominantly in the pet class as a result of being short of features required under the Standard in order to win in shows.

Many of the features mentioned in the preceding chapter are more apparent in the mature Springer than they were in the puppy. Headpiece, neck, back, bone, legs, tail-set, coat, eyes, and teeth as developed in the adult may have improved since puppyhood. But faults observed in the puppy may be more apparent in the adult or new faults may have developed as the puppy progressed toward maturity.

The coat of a mature Springer should be just as described in the Standard: flat or wavy, fine and glossy, indicative of good condition

Ch. Falstaff of Recess

Ch. Cartref Donla's Arpege, C.D.

Ch. Salilyn's Celestial Sally.

(and care). Coat condition is usually helped a great deal by a daily combing.

The pet Springer usually gets the least care and ends up with a curly coat that is often matted, dull, and dead looking. Many owners let the coat go until it is necessary to take the dog someplace to have the hair cut off, which destroys the appearance of the Springer.

In accordance with the Standard, show dogs can be trimmed to enhance the overall picture of the dog. Field dogs are trimmed of all excess feathering to give them the desired clean outline and to save the feathering from becoming tangled and filled with burs.

The coats of liver and white Springers will often sunburn in summer and fade out to become dull, which detracts immensely from the good looks of the dog. If there is shade in the run or the dog is kept inside during sunlight hours, damage to the coat will be lessened. Coats of black and white Springers are not affected in the same way as are those of the liver and white dogs. This is the reason many owners prefer the black and white dogs even though the black sometimes develops a tinge of henna.

The temperament of a typical Springer is described in the Standard as friendly, eager to please, quick to learn, and willing to obey. Well, the breed is said to be the largest lap dog known, and forty-five to sixty pounds of grown dog is really a lapful. But climbing into his owner's lap certainly can be taken as a gesture of friendliness.

Eager to please, quick to learn, and willing to obey—all are terms that are self-explanatory. Still, one must realize that the young dog must be taught what pleases and what constitutes overeagerness. He must be taught how to learn. And he must be taught to obey. Working with the young dog will bring out these traits as well as to eliminate any tendency toward shyness. Excessive timidity and shyness are traits which detract from dogs of any breed, and both are severely penalized universally. They must be avoided at all costs in Springers.

Intelligence in Springers is very marked and many tales have been told to demonstrate just how intelligent this one or that one was. I was told many years ago of the Springer's intelligence and the breed's intelligence is just as marked today as it was then. If you correct a Springer, spank it if you have to, and then forget the misdeed, the dog will seldom make that same mistake again. And it is most interesting to check and keep an account of the number of words your dog seems to understand. The growth of the dog's understanding is most fascinating, and, actually, in many cases it becomes a subject of conversation and even a status symbol. All of these traits must be worked

Sam (Best of Breed), Tolstoy (Best Puppy), and Svetlana (Winners Bitch) at 1968 Eastern English Springer Spaniel Club Speciality Show.

Ch. Charlyle's Holdout

out with each dog individually. But remember, dogs are like children —once they get by with something, it may take a long time to get them back on the track. But that you must do—or suffer the consequences.

Evidence of shyness cannot be ignored but must be dealt with at once. If shyness develops as the puppy grows up, it is a matter of great concern. If you can ascertain the cause, you may be able to eliminate it and control the basic fear which results in shyness. Often, it is impossible to tell just how the fear originates, but shyness usually starts during the dog's formative years and is the result of the owner's neglecting to handle the puppy enough so that it becomes accustomed to humans. Most puppies need to socialize with both people and dogs in order to develop well-balanced personalities.

When checking the Standard, you will note that each section includes a statement concerning penalties if any are to be assessed for deficiencies in the qualities described. Penalties are usually assessed when there can be no question of judgment. This is an attempt to counteract the human element and leave no question as to why the dog does not measure up. In any Springer you acquire—whether for a pet, for showing in the conformation ring, or for use as a gun dog

Ch. Schwedekrest Statesman

Ch. Schwedekrest Sensation

or in field trials—avoid characteristics which are contrary to those required by the Standard, for the faults which are penalized under the Standard will penalize your dog anywhere.

The best advice I have ever heard regarding young dogs is the same as the advice given for children: don't neglect them, even from the first minute. And this advice should be followed for each type of Springer—pet, show, field, or gun dog. Don't neglect the pet just because he is one. You owe it to him to provide a chance at the good life regardless of his status. Don't neglect the show dog or he may go sour and hate shows—and perhaps spook" when exposed to the noise and the commotion that are part of the show game. With the gun dog, whether used for field trialing or hunting, be careful that you don't try to start training too soon, for gunshyness may result if the dog is not properly conditioned before training begins. Gunshyness is really disastrous and usually cannot be cured.

I had two fine Springers that were very good stud dogs and produced fine litters. One sired over one hundred pups and the other between eighty and ninety. Unfortunately, both were gunshy, for they had been taken into the field and handled improperly and shot over without proper conditioning to noise. They had been literally scared into gunshyness.

Open Bitch Class, 1970 Westminster Kennel Club Show.

Ch. Felicia's Matinee Idol.

Viciousness (or meanness in any degree) is another characteristic which should never be fostered in a dog, for it is a trait that can make an outcast of the dog, break its spirit, and also bring trouble to the owner. Vicious dogs do not make good pets, are disqualified as show dogs, and definitely would cause trouble in the field.

The size of the Springer should be in accordance with the provisions of the Standard in order that the dog may perform the work he is intended to do. The Springer should be of a size to fit in at home, to come within the specifications for a show dog, and to cover ground easily in the field.

Legginess in the young dog should be avoided—for sometimes the dog does not outgrow the legginess and ends up either being oversize or too tall for the length of his body. Short legs are equally undesirable, for short legs tend to throw the dog off balance. In addition, a dog with short legs lacks all semblance of quality. A long back is usually a weak one and a too short back restricts gait. The perfect back is one which is approximately equal in length to the height of the dog at the withers. The length of the back is measured from the withers to the base of the tail.

Avoid an oversize head which overbalances the dog. Be sure that the muzzle is parallel to the top of the skull and is neither convex nor concave, and that the head between the ears is twice the width of the muzzle. Make sure that there is no evidence of undershot or overshot bite because either will penalize a show dog and will be very detrimental to a gun dog—for with either defect he will be unable to carry game effectively.

Ch. Dot's It of Marlen

Ch. Marjon's Sparkling Challenge.

Ch. Berlytown Lively Princess, CDX.

Ch. Richmond's Hustler

Grooming the Springer

Grooming is a matter of concern for owners of all Springers—pets, show competitors, and gun dogs—for nothing detracts from a dog's appearance so much as does a lack of care. The Standard states very clearly in the first paragraph that "The English Springer Spaniel is a medium-size sporting dog with a neat compact body and a docked tail. His coat is moderately long, glossy, usually liver and white or black and white with feathering on his legs, ears, chest and brisket."

Under "Color and Coat" the Standard states that "The body coat is flat or wavy, of medium length, sufficiently dense to be water-proof, weather-proof, and thorn-proof. The texture fine and the hair should have the clean, glossy, live appearance indicative of good health. It is legitimate to trim about head, feet, ears; to remove dead hair; to thin and shorten excess feathering particularly from the hocks to the feet and elsewhere as required to give a smart, clean appearance."

If these statements are studied and the requirements fulfilled, they will provide a real foundation for the good grooming which will give your Springer that clean outline which is so desirable in a sporting dog.

Keep your dog looking like a Springer, whatever the role he fills in your life. If he is to be shown in the conformation ring, don't wait until the day before or the day you get to a show to shape up your dog. A small-animal clipper sometimes leaves marks, or you may take off a bit too much. But if the coat has been trimmed a few days before the show, there will be time for the coat to grow sufficiently to look its best.

Trim the Springer according to the Standard. Chances are the breeder you bought him from will be glad to help the first few times. Certainly he would wish to be proud of a dog from his kennel. Or ask a professional handler to trim him up for you—which he will do if he handles the dog at a show.

Trim your gun dog down, taking off most of the feathering and getting the long coat down to a good length so it will be protected in rough going. But do not make it so short that the dog's hide is exposed. Trimming enough to eliminate the possibility the coat will catch burs will help your gun dog work and make the work as enjoyable to him as it is to you. I follow a tip from a hunting companion of former years

and rub some vaseline into the gun dog's coat before taking him into the field. Then the burs and other stickers can be combed out easily.

A well-groomed dog is a status symbol—just as is a clean automobile—so keep your Springer well groomed and get set to fend off the compliments from your friends.

There are numerous lotions that may be applied to give the coat a sheen, but one of the best tonics for a dog's coat is a good brushing —daily, if possible, but at least three times a week.

Liver and white Springers are prone to bleach out after being sunburned. Show dogs, if kept out of the sun, or kept in shade most of the time, will tend to retain the color and the gleam in the coat.

Springers that are allowed to run outside come back to the house covered with swamp muck, dirt, and water. They may look like the "wreck of the Hesperus," but the Springer is one of the few breeds that are "self-cleaning." When Springers dry out, they usually whiten up and shine up all over again. But if the Springer is to be shown, it should have a good bath to remove any accumulation of kennel dust. To set up the coat, bathe the dog, brush the coat thoroughly, and then, by combing or plucking, remove any dead hair that may remain in the coat.

Feet require good care. A pair of curved scissors can be used to trim around each foot, and especially the hair between the toes as well as the hair beneath the foot which sometimes covers the pads. Remember the statement in the Standard—"The feet to be round, or slightly oval, compact, well arched, medium size with thick pads, well feathered between the toes. Excess hair to be removed to show the natural shape and size of the foot." So trim accordingly.

Hair on the legs should be trimmed to give a clean outline and a straight line to the pastern in front, as well as a clean line to the hocks and the rear legs.

Check the nails. If the dog has been running hard on roads or pavement, he may not need a pedicure. Should he require one, be most careful to avoid cutting the quick, for to do so can leave the dog temporarily lame. (See page 38 for specific instructions on nail trimming.)

If you have questions about grooming your Springer, why not watch a handler readying a Springer at a show. Or, as suggested above, ask a professional handler to look your dog over—either to make suggestions or to make repairs to your grooming job. Often, a professional handler will suggest some slight change that improves your dog's appearance materially.

(UPPER LEFT) Wire brush (RIGHT) Bristle brush
(LOWER LEFT) Comb—Hound glove.

They are not "trimmed to pattern," however, as are such longhaired breeds as the Kerry Blue Terrier and the Poodle, which, when shown in the breed ring, must be clipped and trimmed in the patterns specified in the breed Standards.

The Longhaired Dachshund, the Borzoi, and the Yorkshire Terrier have long but comparatively silky coats, whereas the Newfoundland and the Rough Collie have long straight coats with rather harsh texture. Long coats must be kept brushed out thoroughly to eliminate mats and snarls.

The dog should be taught from puppyhood that a grooming session is a time for business, not for play. He should be handled gently, though, for it is essential to avoid hurting him in any way. Grooming time should be pleasant for both dog and master.

Tools required vary with the breed, but always include combs, brushes, and nail clippers and files. Combs should have wide-spaced teeth with rounded ends so that the dog's skin will not be scratched accidentally. For the same reason, brushes with natural bristles are usually preferable to those with synthetic bristles that may be too fine and sharp.

A light, airy, pleasant place in which to work is desirable, and it is of the utmost importance that neither dog nor master be

*Grooming and
General Coat Care*

Although coat types, textures, and patterns may seem purely arbitrary matters of little consequence, they are among the important characteristics that distinguish one breed from another. Actually, each breed has been developed to serve a specific purpose, and the coat that is considered typical for the breed is also the one most appropriate for the dog's specialized use—be it as guard, hunting companion, herder, or pet. A knowledge of the breed Standard approved by The American Kennel Club is helpful to the owner who takes pride in owning a well-groomed dog, typical of its breed.

Dogs with short, smooth coats (such as the Weimaraner, Basset, Beagle, smooth Dachshund and Chihuahua) usually shed only moderately and their coats require little routine grooming other than thorough brushing with a bristle brush or hound glove. For exhibition in the show ring, the whiskers, or "feelers," are trimmed close to the muzzle, but no other trimming is needed.

The wire coat of the Airedale, Wire Fox Terrier, Miniature Schnauzer, or Wirehaired Dachshund should be stripped or plucked in show trim at regular intervals. The dog can then be kept well groomed by thorough combing and brushing.

Curly coated breeds such as the Curly Coated Retriever, and the American and Irish Water Spaniels, generally require no special coat care other than frequent brushing. True curly coated breeds are very curly indeed and are not to be confused with breeds such as the Golden Retriever, Gordon Setter, Brittany Spaniel, and English Springer Spaniel, which have slightly curled or wavy coats of somewhat silky texture. The longer hair, or "feathers," typically found on tail, legs, ears, and chest of these breeds should be trimmed slightly to make the outline neater.

Ch. Beryltown Bold Crusader, bred by Beryl Hines, owned by Earl Taisey, and handled by Bobby Barlow.

Ch. Beryltown Screaming Rocket, C.D., owned by John Grill and Beryl Hines, and campaigned by Robert Walgate.

Spot, before grooming.

Possibly it is a question of ears being too close to the head, or less than ideal tail-set, back line, feet, stop, or neck. A professional handler or a serious breeder can show you how to groom your Springer so that less desirable aspects are not so obvious.

Remember that the Standard provides penalties for "Over-trimming, especially of the body coat. Any chopped, barbered or artificial effect. Excessive feathering that destroys the clean outline desirable in a sporting dog." Yes, the art of trimming should be studied, and the trimming should be done with restraint and with knowledge of what results are most desirable.

Before you attempt to trim a puppy for the first time, turn on the clippers while you handle the puppy. Hold the puppy until he quiets down and pays no attention to the noise. Gradually edge the dog closer to the clipper until you can slide the clipper up and down the puppy's spine. Finally, take a wisp of hair off the head or the neck. Then continue with the introduction to the clipper. Eventually, go ahead and trim the dog. Do the head, neck, and throat the first time. But be prepared to stop if the puppy refuses to be quiet while you work on him. Then start again—and be patient. By introducing the puppy to the clipper gradually, you should be able to avoid trouble in the future—which is highly desirable. Being unafraid of the clipper is a valuable asset for any Springer puppy and will usually continue for life.

Spot, after grooming.

distracted by other dogs, cats, or people. Consequently, it is usually preferable that grooming be done indoors.

Particularly for large or medium breeds, a sturdy grooming table is desirable. Many owners hold small puppies or Toy dogs during grooming sessions, athough it is better if they, too, are groomed on a table. Large and medium size dogs should be taught to jump onto the table and to jump off again when grooming is completed. Small dogs must be lifted on and off to avoid falls and possible injury. The dog should stand while the back and upper portions of the body are groomed, and lie on his side while underparts of his body are brushed, nails clipped, etc.

Before each session, the dog should be permitted to relieve himself. Once grooming is begun, it is important to avoid keeping the dog standing so long that he becomes tired. If a good deal of grooming is needed, it should be done in two or more short periods.

It is almost impossible to brush too much, and show dogs are often brushed for a full half hour a day, year round. If you cannot brush your dog every day, you should brush him a minimum of two or three times a week. Brushing removes loose skin particles and stimulates circulation, thereby improving condition of the skin. It also stimulates secretion of the natural skin oils that make the coat look healthy and beautiful.

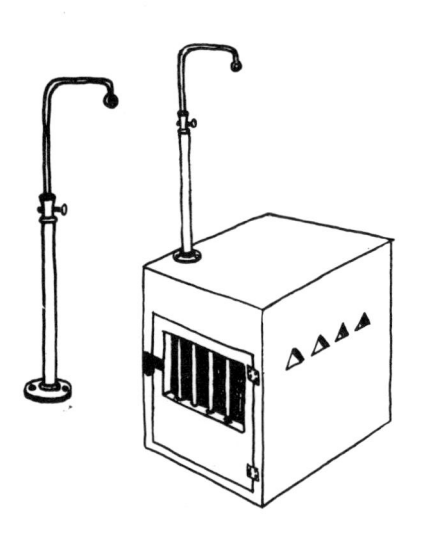

Dog crate with grooming—table top is ideal—providing rigid, well supported surface on which to groom dog, and serving as indoor kennel for puppy or grown dog. Rubber matting provides non-slip surface. Dog's collar may be attached to adjustable arm. Lightweight and readily transported yet sturdy, the crate is especially useful to owner who takes dog with him when he travels.

Before brushing, any burs adhering to the coat, as well as matted hair, should be carefully removed, using the fingers and coarse toothed comb with a gentle, teasing motion to avoid tearing the coat. The coat should first be brushed lightly in the direction in which the hair grows. Next, it should be brushed vigorously in the opposite direction, a small portion at a time, making sure the bristles penetrate the hair to the skin, until the entire coat has been brushed thoroughly and all loose soil removed. Then the coat should be brushed in the direction the hair grows, until every hair is sleekly in place.

The dog that is kept well brushed needs bathing only rarely. Once or twice a year is usually enough. Except for unusual circumstances when his coat becomes excessively soiled, no puppy under six months of age should be bathed in water. If it is necessary to bathe a puppy, extreme care must be exercised so that he will not become chilled. No dog should be bathed during cold weather and then permitted to go outside immediately. Whatever the weather, the dog should always be given a good run outdoors and permitted to relieve himself before he is bathed.

Various types of "dry baths" are available at pet supply stores. In general, they are quite satisfactory when circumstances are such that a bath in water is impractical. Dry shampoos are usually rubbed into the dog's coat thoroughly, then removed by vigorous towelling or brushing.

Before starting a water bath, the necessary equipment should be assembled. This includes a tub of appropriate size, and another tub or pail for rinse water. (A small hose with a spray nozzle—one that may be attached to the water faucet—is ideal for rinsing the dog.) A metal or plastic cup for dipping water, special dog shampoo, a small bottle of mineral or olive oil, and a supply of absorbent cotton should be placed nearby, as well as a supply of heavy towels, a wash cloth, and the dog's combs and brushes.

The amount of water required will vary according to the size of the dog, but should reach no higher than the dog's elbows. Bath water and rinse water should be slightly warmer than lukewarm, but should not be hot.

To avoid accidentally getting water in the dog's ears, place a small amount of absorbent cotton in each. With the dog standing in the tub, wet his body by using the cup to pour water over

him. Take care to avoid wetting the head, and be careful to avoid getting water or shampoo in the eyes. (If you should accidentally do so, placing a few drops of mineral or olive oil in the inner corner of the eye will bring relief.) When the dog is thoroughly wet, put a small amount of shampoo on his back and work up a lather, rubbing briskly. Wash his entire body and then rinse as much of the shampoo as possible from the coat by dipping water from the tub and pouring it over the dog.

Dip the wash cloth into clean water, wring it out enough so it won't drip, then wash the dog's head, taking care to avoid the eyes. Remove the cotton from the dog's ears and sponge them gently, inside and out. Shampoo should never be used inside the ears, so if they are extremely soiled, sponge them clean with cotton saturated with mineral or olive oil. (Between baths, the ears should be cleaned frequently in the same way.)

Replace the cotton in the ears, then use the cup and container of rinse water (or hose and spray nozzle) to rinse the dog thoroughly. Quickly wrap a towel around him, remove him from the tub, and towel him as dry as possible. To avoid getting an impromptu bath yourself, you must act quickly, for once he is out of the tub, the dog will instinctively shake himself.

While the hair is still slightly damp, use a clean comb or brush to remove any tangles. If the hair is allowed to dry first, it may be completely impossible to remove them.

So far as routine grooming is concerned, the dog's eyes require little attention. Some dogs have a slight accumulation of mucus in the corner of the eyes upon waking mornings. A salt solution (1 teaspoon of table salt to one pint of warm, sterile water) can be sponged around the eyes to remove the stain. During grooming sessions it is well to inspect the eyes, since many breeds are prone to eye injury. Eye problems of a minor nature may be treated at home (see page 50), but it is imperative that any serious eye abnormality be called to the attention of the veterinarian immediately.

Feeding hard dog biscuits and hard bones helps to keep tooth surfaces clean. Slight discoloration may be readily removed by rubbing with a damp cloth dipped in salt or baking soda. The dog's head should be held firmly, the lips pulled apart gently, and the teeth rubbed lightly with the dampened cloth. Regular

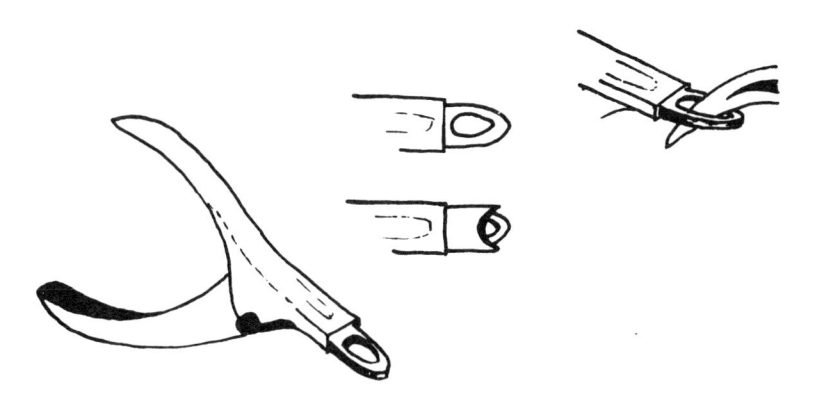

Nail trimmer—center detail shows blade cutting action. Right shows manner of inserting nail in cutter.

care usually keeps the teeth in good condition, but if tartar accumulates, it should be removed by a veterinarian.

If the dog doesn't keep his nails worn down through regular exercise on hard surfaces, they must be trimmed at intervals, for nails that are too long may cause the foot to spread and thus spoil the dog's gait. Neglected nails may even grow so long that they will grow into a circle and puncture the dog's skin. Nails can be cut easily with a nail trimmer that slides over the nail end. The cut is made just outside the faintly pink bloodline that can be seen on white nails. In pigmented nails, the bloodline is not easily seen, so the cut should be made just outside the hooklike projection on the underside of the nails. A few downward strokes with a nail file will smooth the cut surface, and, once shortened, nails can be kept short by filing at regular intervals.

Care must be taken that nails are not cut too short, since blood vessels may be accidentally severed. Should you accidentally cut a nail so short that it bleeds, apply a mild antiseptic and keep the dog quiet until bleeding stops. Usually, only a few drops of blood will be lost. But once a dog's nails have been cut painfully short, he will usually object when his feet are handled.

Nutrition

The main food elements required by dogs are proteins, fats, and carbohydrates. Vitamins A, B complex, D, and E are essential, as are ample amounts of calcium and iron. Nine other minerals are required in small amounts but are amply provided in almost any diet, so there is no need to be concerned about them.

The most important nutrient is protein and it must be provided every day of the dog's life, for it is essential for normal daily growth and replacement of body tissues burned up in daily activity. Preferred animal protein products are beef, mutton, horse meat, and boned fish. Visceral organs—heart, liver, and tripe—are good but if used in too large quantities may cause diarrhea (bones in large amounts have the same effect). Pork, particularly fat pork, is undesirable. The "meat meal" used in some commercial foods is made from scrap meat processed at high temperatures and then dried. It is not quite so nutritious as fresh meat, but in combination with other protein products, it is an acceptable ingredient in the dog's diet.

Cooked eggs and raw egg yolk are good sources of protein, but raw egg white should never be fed since it cannot be digested by the dog and may cause diarrhea. Cottage cheese and milk (fresh, dried, and canned) are high in protein, also. Puppies thrive on milk and it can well be included in the diet of older dogs, too, if mixed with meat, vegetables, and meal. Soy-bean meal, wheat germ meal, and dried brewers yeast are vegetable products high in protein and may be used to advantage in the diet.

Vegetable and animal fats in moderate amounts should be used, especially if a main ingredient of the diet is dry or kibbled food. Fats should not be used excessively or the dog may become overweight. Generally, fats should be increased slightly in the winter and reduced somewhat during warm weather.

Carbohydrates are required for proper assimilation of fats. Dog biscuits, kibble, dog meal, and other dehydrated foods are good sources of carbohydrates, as are cereal products derived from rice, corn, wheat, and ground or rolled oats.

Vegetables supply additional proteins, vitamins, and minerals, and by providing bulk are of value in overcoming constipation. Raw or cooked carrots, celery, lettuce, beets, asparagus, tomatoes, and cooked spinach may be used. They should always be chopped or ground well and mixed with the other food. Various combinations may be used, but a good home-mixed ration for the mature dog consists of two parts of meat and one each of vegetables and dog meal (or cereal product).

Dicalcium phosphate and cod-liver oil are added to puppy diets to ensure inclusion of adequate amounts of calcium and Vitamins A and D. Indiscriminate use of dietary supplements is not only unjustified but may actually be harmful and many breeders feel that their over-use in diets of extremely small breeds may lead to excessive growth as well as to overweight at maturity.

Foods manufactured by well-known and reputable food processors are nutritionally sound and are offered in sufficient variety of flavors, textures, and consistencies that most dogs will find them tempting and satisfying. Canned foods are usually "ready to eat," while dehydrated foods in the form of kibble, meal, or biscuits may require the addition of water or milk. Dried foods containing fat sometimes become rancid, so to avoid an unpalatable change in flavor, the manufacturer may not include fat in dried food but recommend its addition at the time the water or milk is added.

Candy and other sweets are taboo, for the dog has no nutritional need for them and if he is permitted to eat them, he will usually eat less of foods he requires. Also taboo are fried foods, highly seasoned foods and extremely starchy foods, for the dog's digestive tract is not equipped to handle them.

Frozen foods should be thawed completely and warmed at least to lukewarm, while hot foods should be cooled to lukewarm. Food should be in a fairly firm state, for sloppy food is difficult for the dog to digest.

Whether meat is raw or cooked makes little difference, so long as the dog is also given the juice that seeps from the meat during cooking. Bones provide little nourishment, although gnawing bones helps make the teeth strong and helps to keep tartar from accumulating on them. Beef bones, especially large knuckle bones, are best. Fish, poultry, and chop bones should never be

given to dogs since they have a tendency to splinter and may puncture the dog's digestive tract.

Clean, fresh, cool water is essential to all dogs and an adequate supply should be readily available twenty-four hours a day from the time the puppy is big enough to walk. Especially during hot weather, the drinking pan should be emptied and refilled at frequent intervals.

Puppies usually are weaned by the time they are six weeks old, so when you acquire a new puppy ten to twelve weeks old, he will already have been started on a feeding schedule. The breeder should supply exact details as to number of meals per day, types and amounts of food offered, etc. It is essential to adhere to this established routine, for drastic changes in diet may produce intestinal upsets.

Until a puppy is six months old, milk formula is an integral part of the diet. A day's supply should be made up at one time and stored in the refrigerator, and the quantity needed for each meal warmed at feeding time. The following combination is good for all breeds:

1 pint whole fresh milk	1 tablespoon lime water
1 raw egg yolk, slightly beaten	1 tablespoon lactose

The two latter items (as well as cod-liver oil and dicalcium phosphate to be added to solid food) are readily available at pet supply stores and drug stores.

At twelve weeks of age the amount of formula given at each feeding will vary from three to four tablespoonfuls for the Toy breeds, to perhaps two cupfuls for the large breeds. If the puppy is on the five-meal-a-day schedule when he leaves the kennel, three of the meals (first, third, and fifth each day) should consist of formula only. On a four-meal schedule, the first and fourth meals should be formula.

In either case, the second meal of the day should consist of chopped beef (preferably raw). The amount needed will vary from about three tablespoonfuls for Toy breeds up to one-half cupful for large breeds. The other meal should consist of equal parts of chopped beef and strained, cooked vegetables to which is added a little dry toast. (If you plan eventually to feed your dog canned food or dog meal, it can gradually be introduced at this

meal.) Cod-liver oil and dicalcium phosphate should be mixed with the food for this meal. The amount of each will vary from one-half teaspoonful for Toys to 1 tablespoonful for large breeds.

The amount of food offered at each meal must gradually be increased and by five months the puppy will require about twice what he needed at three months. Puppies should be fat, and it is best to let them eat as much as they want at each meal, so long as they are hungry again when it is time for the next feeding. Any food not eaten within fifteen minutes should be taken away. With a little attention to the dog's eating habits, the owner can prepare enough food and still not waste any.

When the puppy is five months old, the final feeding of the day can be eliminated and the five meals compressed into four so the puppy still receives the same quantities and types of food. At six or seven months, the four meals can be compressed into three. By the time a puppy of small or medium breed is eleven to twelve months old, feedings can be reduced to two meals a day. At the end of the first year, cod-liver oil and dicalcium phosphate can usually be discontinued.

Large breeds mature more slowly and three meals a day are usually necessary until eighteen or twenty-four months of age. Cod-liver oil and dicalcium phosphate should be continued, too, until the large dog reaches maturity.

A mature dog usually eats slightly less than he did as a growing puppy. For mature dogs, one large meal a day is usually sufficient, although some owners prefer to give two meals. As long as the dog enjoys optimum health and is neither too fat nor too thin, the number of meals a day makes little difference.

The amount of food required for mature dogs will vary. With canned dog food or home-prepared foods (that is, the combination of meat, vegetables, and meal), the approximate amount required is one-half ounce of food per pound of body weight. Thus, about eight ounces of such foods would be needed each day for a mature dog weighing sixteen pounds. If the dog is fed a dehydrated commercial food, approximately one ounce of food is needed for each pound of body weight. Approximately one pound of dry food per day would be required by a dog weighing sixteen pounds. Most manufacturers of commercial foods provide information on packages as to approximate daily needs of various breeds.

As a dog becomes older and less active, he may become too fat. Or his appetite may decrease so he becomes too thin. It is necessary to adjust the diet in either case, for the dog will live longer and enjoy better health if he is maintained in trim condition. The simplest way to decrease or increase body weight is by decreasing or increasing the amount of fat in the diet. Protein content should be maintained at a high level throughout the dog's life, although the amount of food at each meal can be decreased if the dog becomes too fat.

If the older dog becomes reluctant to eat, it may be necessary to coax him with special food he normally relishes. Warming the food will increase its aroma and usually will help to entice the dog to eat. If he still refuses, rubbing some of the food on the dog's lips and gums may stimulate interest. It may be helpful also to offer food in smaller amounts and increase the number of meals per day. Foods that are highly nutritious and easily digested are especially desirable for older dogs. Small amounts of cooked, ground liver, cottage cheese, or mashed, hard-cooked eggs should be included in the diet often.

Before a bitch is bred, her owner should make sure that she is in optimum condition—slightly on the lean side rather than fat. The bitch in whelp is given much the same diet she was fed prior to breeding, with slight increases in amounts of meat, liver, and dairy products. Beginning about six weeks after breeding, she should be fed two meals per day rather than one, and the total daily intake increased. (Some bitches in whelp require as much as 50% more food than they consume normally.) She must not be permitted to become fat, for whelping problems are more likely to occur in overweight dogs. Cod-liver oil and dicalcium phosphate should be provided until after the puppies are weaned. The amount of each will vary from one-half teaspoonful to one tablespoonful a day, depending upon her size.

The dog used only occasionally for breeding will not require a special diet, but he should be well fed and maintained in optimum condition. A dog that is at public stud and used frequently may require a slightly increased amount of food. But his basic diet will require no change so long as his general health is good and his flesh is firm and hard.

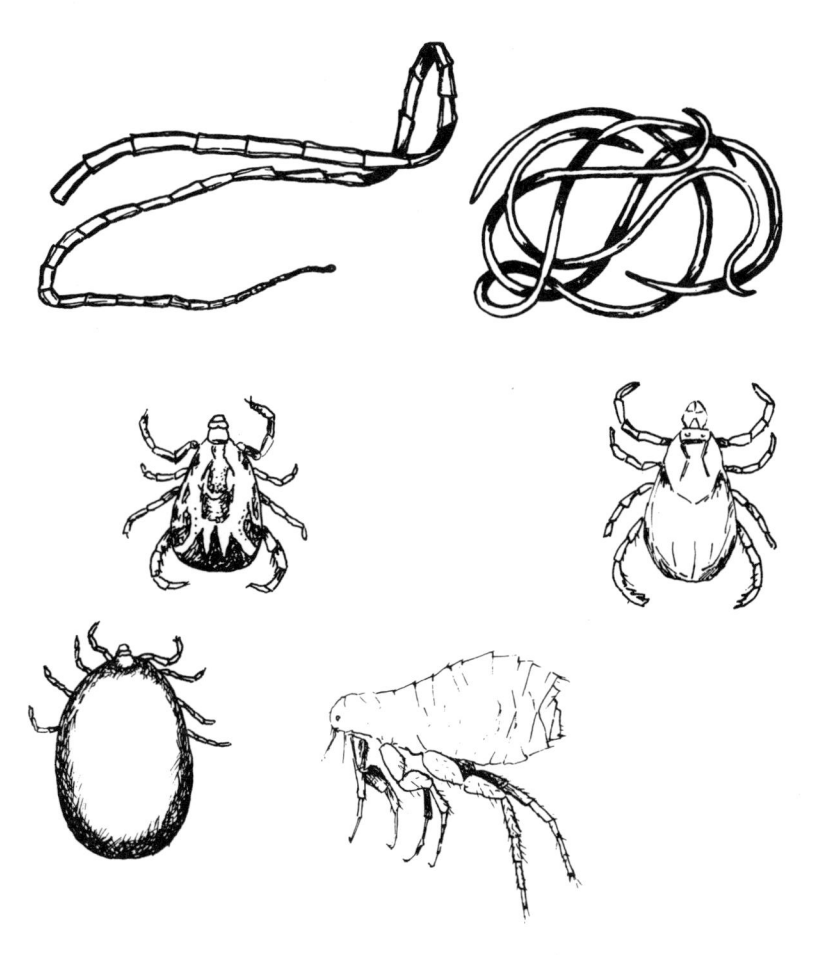

Some common internal and external parasites.

(UPPER LEFT) Tape worm. (UPPER RIGHT) Round worms. (CENTER) American dog ticks—left, female and right, male (much enlarged). (LOWER LEFT) Female tick engorged. (LOWER RIGHT) dog flea (much enlarged).

Maintaining the Dog's Health

Proper nutrition is essential in maintaining the dog's resistance to infectious diseases, in reducing susceptibility to organic diseases, and, of course, in preventing dietary deficiency diseases.

Rickets is probably the most common deficiency disease and afflicts puppies not provided sufficient calcium and Vitamin D. Bones fail to calcify properly, development of teeth is retarded, joints become knobby and deformed, and muscles are flabby. Symptoms include lameness, arching of neck and back, and a tendency of the legs to bow. Treatment consists of providing adequate amounts of dicalcium phosphate and Vitamin D and exposing the dog to sunlight. If detected and treated before reaching an advanced stage, bone damage may be lessened somewhat, although it cannot be corrected completely.

Osteomalacia, similar to rickets, may occur in adult dogs. Treatment is the same as for rickets, but here, too, prevention is preferable to cure. Permanent deformities resulting from rickets or osteomalacia will not be inherited, so once victims recover, they can be used for breeding.

To prevent the growth of disease-producing bacteria and other micro-organisms, cleanliness is essential. All equipment, especially water and food dishes, must be kept immaculately clean. Cleanliness is also essential in controlling external parasites, which thrive in unsanitary surroundings.

Fleas, lice, mites, and ticks can be eradicated in the dog's quarters by regular use of one of the insecticide sprays with a four to six weeks' residual effect. Bedding, blankets, and pillows should be laundered frequently and treated with an insecticide containing rotenone or DDT. Treatment for external parasites varies, depending upon the parasite involved, but a number of good dips and powders are available at pet stores.

Fleas may be eliminated by using a flea powder containing lindane. The coat must be dusted thoroughly with the powder at frequent intervals during the summer months when fleas are

a problem. For eradicating lice, dips containing rotenone or DDT must be applied to the coat. A fine-toothed comb should then be used to remove dead lice and eggs, which are firmly attached to the coat. Mites live deep in the ear canal, producing irritation to the lining of the ear and causing a brownish-black, dry type discharge. Plain mineral oil or ear ointment should be swabbed on the inner surface of the ear twice a week until mites are eliminated. Ticks may carry Rocky Mountain spotted fever, so, to avoid possible infection, they should be removed from the dog only with tweezers and should be destroyed by burning (or by dropping them into insecticide). Heavy infestation can be controlled by sponging the coat daily with a solution containing a special tick dip.

Among preparations available for controlling parasites on the dog's body are some that can be given internally. Since dosage must be carefully controlled, these preparations should not be used without consulting a veterinarian.

Internal parasites, with the exception of the tapeworm, may be transmitted from a mother dog to the puppies. Infestation may also result from contact with infected bedding or through access to a yard where an infected dog relieves himself. The types that may infest dogs are roundworms, whipworms, tapeworms, hookworms, and heartworms. All cause similar symptoms: a generally unthrifty appearance, stary coat, dull eyes, weakness and emaciation despite a ravenous appetite, coughing, vomiting, diarrhea, and sometimes bloody stools. Not all symptoms are present in every case, of course.

Promiscuous dosing for worms is dangerous and different types of worms require different treatment. So if you suspect your dog has worms, ask your veterinarian to make a microscopic examination of the feces, and to prescribe appropriate treatment if evidence of worm infestation is found.

Clogged anal glands cause intense discomfort, which the dog may attempt to relieve by scooting himself along the floor on his haunches. These glands, located on either side of the anus, secrete a substance that enables the dog to expel the contents of the rectum. If they become clogged, they may give the dog an unpleasant odor and when neglected, serious infection may result. Contents of the glands can be easily expelled into a wad of

cotton, which should be held under the tail with the left hand. Then, using the right hand, pressure should be exerted with the thumb on one side of the anus, the forefinger on the other. The normal secretion is brownish in color, with an unpleasant odor. The presence of blood or pus indicates infection and should be called to the attention of a veterinarian.

Fits, often considered a symptom of worms, may result from a variety of causes, including vitamin deficiencies, or playing to the point of exhaustion. A veterinarian should be consulted when a fit occurs, for it may be a symptom of serious illness.

Distemper takes many and varied forms, so it is sometimes difficult for even experienced veterinarians to diagnose. It is the number one killer of dogs, and although it is not unknown in older dogs, its victims are usually puppies. While some dogs do recover, permanent damage to the brain or nervous system is often sustained. Symptoms may include lethargy, diarrhea, vomiting, reduced appetite, cough, nasal discharge, inflammation of the eyes, and a rise in temperature. If distemper is suspected, a veterinarian must be consulted at once, for early treatment is essential. Effective preventive measures lie in inoculation. Shots for temporary immunity should be given all puppies within a few weeks after whelping, and the permanent inoculations should be given as soon thereafter as possible.

Hardpad has been fairly prevalent in Great Britain for a number of years, and its incidence in the United States is increasing. Symptoms are similar to those of distemper, but as the disease progresses, the pads of the feet harden and eventually peel. Chances of recovery are not favorable unless prompt veterinary care is secured.

Infectious hepatitis in dogs affects the liver, as does the human form, but apparently is not transmissible to man. Symptoms are similar to those of distemper, and the disease rapidly reaches the acute stage. Since hepatitis is often fatal, prompt veterinary treatment is essential. Effective vaccines are available and should be provided all puppies. A combination distemper-hepatitis vaccine is sometimes used.

Leptospirosis is caused by a micro-organism often transmitted by contact with rats, or by ingestion of food contaminated by rats. The disease can be transmitted to man, so anyone caring for an afflicted dog must take steps to avoid infection. Symptoms include vomiting, loss of appetite, diarrhea, fever, depression and lethargy, redness of eyes and gums, and sometimes jaundice. Since permanent kidney damage may result, veterinary treatment should be secured immediately.

Rabies is a disease that is always fatal—and it is transmissible to man. It is caused by a virus that attacks the nervous system and is present in the saliva of an infected animal. When an infected animal bites another, the virus is transmitted to the new victim. It may also enter the body through cuts and scratches that come in contact with saliva containing the virus.

All warm-blooded animals are subject to rabies and it may be transmitted by foxes, skunks, squirrels, horses, and cattle as well as dogs. Anyone bitten by a dog (or other animal) should see his physician immediately, and health and law enforcement officials should be notified. Also, if your dog is bitten by another animal, consult your veterinarian immediately.

In most areas, rabies shots are required by law. Even if not required, all dogs should be given anti-rabies vaccine, for it is an effective preventive measure.

Injuries of a serious nature—deep cuts, broken bones, severe burns, etc.—always require veterinary care. However, the dog may need first aid before being moved to a veterinary hospital.

A dog injured in any way should be approached cautiously, for reactions of a dog in pain are unpredictable and he may bite even a beloved master. A muzzle should always be applied before any attempt is made to move the dog or treat him in any way. The muzzle can be improvised from a strip of cloth, bandage, or even heavy cord, looped firmly around the dog's jaws and tied under the lower jaw. The ends should then be extended back of the neck and tied again so the loop around the jaws will stay in place.

A stretcher for moving a heavy dog can be improvised from a rug or board—preferably two people should be available to transport it. A small dog can be carried by one person simply by grasping the loose skin at the nape of the neck with one hand and placing the other hand under the dog's hips.

Severe bleeding from a leg can be controlled by applying a tourniquet between the wound and the body, but the tourniquet must be loosened at ten-minute intervals. Severe bleeding from head or body can be controlled by placing a cloth or gauze pad over the wound, then applying firm pressure with the hand.

To treat minor cuts, first trim the hair from around the wound, then wash the area with warm soapy water and apply a mild antiseptic such as tincture of metaphen.

Shock is usually the aftermath of severe injury and requires immediate veterinary attention. The dog appears dazed, lips and tongue are pale, and breathing is shallow. The dog should be wrapped in blankets and kept warm, and if possible, kept lying down with his head lower than his body.

Fractures require immediate professional attention. A broken bone should be immobilized while the dog is transported to the veterinarian but no attempt should be made to splint it.

Burns from hot liquid or hot metals should be treated by applying a bland ointment, provided the burned area is small. Burns over large areas should be treated by a veterinarian.

Burns from chemicals should first be treated by flushing the coat with plain water, taking care to protect the dog's eyes and ears. A baking soda solution can then be applied to neutralize the chemical further. If the burned area is small, a bland ointment should be applied. If the burned area is large, more extensive treatment will be required, as well as veterinary care.

Poisoning is more often accidental than deliberate, but whichever the case, symptoms and treatment are the same. If the poisoning is not discovered immediately, the dog may be found unconscious. His mouth will be slimy, he will tremble, have difficulty breathing, and possibly go into convulsions. Veterinary treatment must be secured immediately.

If you find the dog eating something you know to be poisonous, induce vomiting immediately by repeatedly forcing the dog to swallow a mixture of equal parts of hydrogen peroxide and water. Delay of even a few minutes may result in death. When the contents of the stomach have been emptied, force the dog to swallow raw egg white, which will slow absorption of the poison. Then call the veterinarian. Provide him with information as to the type of poison, and follow his advice as to further treatment.

Some chemicals are toxic even though not swallowed, so before using a product, make sure it can be used safely around pets.

Electric shock usually results because an owner negligently leaves an electric cord exposed where the dog can chew on it. If possible, disconnect the cord before touching the dog. Otherwise, yank the cord from the dog's mouth so you will not receive a shock when you try to help him. If the dog is unconscious, artificial respiration and stimulants will be required, so a veterinarian should be consulted at once.

Eye problems of a minor nature—redness or occasional discharge—may be treated with a few drops of boric acid solution (2%) or salt solution (1 teaspoonful table salt to 1 pint sterile water). Cuts on the eyeball, bruises close to the eyes, or persistent discharge shoud be treated only by a veterinarian.

Skin problems usually cause persistent itching. However, *follicular mange* does not usually do so but is evidenced by moth-eaten-looking patches, especially about the head and along the back. *Sarcoptic mange* produces severe itching and is evidenced by patchy, crusty areas on body, legs, and abdomen. Any evidence suggesting either should be called to the attention of a veterinarian. Both require extensive treatment and both may be contracted by humans.

Eczema is characterized by extreme itching, redness of the skin and exudation of serous matter. It may result from a variety

of causes, and the exact cause in a particular case may be difficult to determine. Relief may be secured by dusting the dog twice a week with a soothing powder containing a fungicide and an insecticide.

Allergies are not readily distinguished from other skin troubles except through laboratory tests. However, dog owners should be alert to the fact that straw, shavings, or newspapers used for bedding, various coat dressings and shampoos, or simply bathing the dog too often, may produce allergic skin reactions in some dogs. Thus, a change in dog-keeping practices often relieves them.

Symptoms of illness may be so obvious there is no question that the dog is ill, or so subtle that the owner isn't sure whether there is a change from normal or not. *Loss of appetite, malaise* (general lack of interest in what is going on), *and vomiting* may be ignored if they occur singly and persist only for a day. However, in combination with other evidence of illness, such symptoms may be significant and the dog should be watched closely. *Abnormal bowel movements,* especially diarrhea or bloody stools, are cause for immediate concern. *Urinary abnormalities* may indicate infections, and bloody urine is always an indication of a serious condition. When a dog that has long been housebroken suddenly becomes incontinent, a veterinarian should be consulted, for he may be able to suggest treatment or medication that will be helpful.

Persistent coughing is often considered a symptom of worms, but may also indicate heart trouble—especially in older dogs.

Vomiting is another symptom often attributed to worm infestation. Dogs suffering from indigestion sometimes eat grass, apparently to induce vomiting and relieve discomfort.

Stary coat—dull and lackluster—indicates generally poor health and possible worm infestation. *Dull eyes* may result from similar conditions. Certain forms of blindness may also cause the eyes to lose the sparkle of vibrant good health.

Fever is a positive indication of illness and consistent deviation from the normal temperature range of 100 to 102 degrees is cause for concern. To take the dog's temperature, first place the dog on his side. Coat the bulb of a rectal thermometer with petroleum jelly, raise the dog's tail, insert the thermometer to approximately

half its length, and hold it in position for two minutes. Clean the thermometer with rubbing alcohol after each use and be sure to shake it down.

A dog that is seriously ill, requiring surgical treatment, transfusions, or intravenous feeding, must be hospitalized. One requiring less complicated treatment is better cared for at home, but it is essential that the dog be kept in a quiet environment. Preferably, his bed should be in a room apart from family activity, yet close at hand, so his condition can be checked frequently. Clean bedding and adequate warmth are essential, as are a constant supply of fresh, cool water, and foods to tempt the appetite.

Special equipment is not ordinarily needed, but the following items will be useful in caring for a sick dog, as well as in giving first aid for injuries:

petroleum jelly	tincture of metaphen
rubbing alcohol	cotton, gauze, and adhesive tape
mineral oil	burn ointment
rectal thermometer	tweezers
hydrogen peroxide	boric acid solution (2%)

If special medication is prescribed, it may be administered in any one of several ways. A pill or small capsule may be concealed in a small piece of meat, which the dog will usually swallow with no problem. A large capsule may be given by holding the dog's mouth open, inserting the capsule as far as possible down the throat, then holding the mouth closed until the dog swallows. Liquid medicine should be measured into a small bottle or test tube. Then, if the corner of the dog's lip is pulled out while the head is tilted upward, the liquid can be poured between the lips and teeth, a small amount at a time. If he refuses to swallow, keeping the dog's head tilted and stroking his throat will usually induce swallowing.

Foods offered the sick dog should be particularly nutritious and easily digested. Meals should be smaller than usual and offered at more frequent intervals. If the dog is reluctant to eat, offer food he particularly likes and warm it slightly to increase aroma and thus make it more tempting.

Housing Your Dog

Every dog should have a bed of his own, snug and warm, where he can retire undisturbed when he wishes to nap. And, especially with a small puppy, it is desirable to have the bed arranged so the dog can be securely confined at times, safe and contented. If the puppy is taught early in life to stay quietly in his box at night, or when the family is out, the habit will carry over into adulthood and will benefit both dog and master.

The dog should never be banished to a damp, cold basement, but should be quartered in an out-of-the-way corner close to the center of family activity. His bed can be an elaborate cushioned affair with electric warming pad, or simply a rectangular wooden box or heavy paper carton, cushioned with a clean cotton rug or towel. Actually, the latter is ideal for a new puppy, for it is snug, easy to clean, and expendable. A "door" can be cut on one side of the box for easy access, but it should be placed in such a way that the dog can still be confined when desirable.

The shipping crates used by professional handlers at dog shows make ideal indoor quarters. They are lightweight but strong, provide adequate air circulation, yet are snug and warm and easily cleaned. For the dog owner who takes his dog along when he travels, a dog crate is ideal, for the dog will willingly stay in his accustomed bed during long automobile trips, and the crate can be taken inside motels or hotels at night, making the dog a far more acceptable guest.

Dog crates are made of chromed metal or wood, and some have tops covered with a special rubber matting so they can be used as grooming tables. Anyone moderately handy with tools can construct a crate similar to the one illustrated on page 35.

Crates come in various sizes, to suit various breeds of dogs. For reasons of economy, the size selected for a puppy should be adequate for use when the dog is full grown. If the area seems too large when the puppy is small, a temporary cardboard partition can be installed to limit the area he occupies.

The dog owner who lives in the suburbs or in the country may want to keep a mature dog outdoors part of the time, in which case an outdoor doghouse should be provided. This type of kennel can also be constructed by the home handyman, but must be more substantial than quarters used indoors.

Outside finish of the doghouse can be of any type, but double wall construction will make for greater warmth in chilly weather. The floor should be smooth and easy to clean, so tongued and grooved boards or plywood are best. To keep the floor from contact with the damp earth, supports should be laid flat on the ground, running lengthwise of the structure. 2 x 4s serve well as supports for doghouses for small or medium breeds, but 4 x 4s should be used for large breeds.

The outdoor kennel must be big enough so that the dog can turn around inside, but small enough so that his body heat will keep it warm in chilly weather. The overall length of the kennel shoud be twice the length of the adult dog, measured from tip of nose to onset of tail. Width of the structure should be approximately three-fourths the length. And height from the floor to the point where the roof begins should be approximately one and a half the adult dog's height at the shoulders. If you build the house when the dog is still a puppy, you can determine his approximate adult size by referring to the Standard for his breed.

An "A" type roof is preferable, and an overhang of six inches all the way around will provide protection from sun and rain. If the roof is hinged to fold back, the interior of the kennel can be cleaned readily.

The entrance should be placed to one side rather than in the center, which will provide further protection against the weather. One of the commercially made door closures of rubber will keep out rain, snow, and wind, yet give the pet complete freedom to enter and leave his home.

The best location for the doghouse is where it will get enough morning sun to keep it dry, yet will not be in full sun during hot afternoons. If possible, the back of the doghouse should be placed toward the prevailing winds.

A fenced run or yard is essential to the outdoor kennel, and the fence must be sturdy enough that the dog cannot break through it, and high enough so he cannot jump or climb over it. The gate should have a latch of a type that can't be opened accidentally. The area enclosed must provide the dog with space to exercise freely, or else the dog must be exercised on the leash every day, for no dog should be confined to a tiny yard day after day without adequate exercise.

The yard must be kept clean and odor free, and the doghouse must be scrubbed and disinfected at frequent intervals. One of the insecticides made especially for use in kennels—one with a four to six weeks' residual effect—should be used regularly on floors and walls, inside and out.

Enough bedding must be provided so the dog can snuggle into it and keep warm in chilly weather. Bedding should either be of a type that is inexpensive, so it can be discarded and replaced frequently, or of a type that can be laundered readily. Dogs are often allergic to fungi found on straw, hay, or grass, and sometimes newspaper ink, but cedar shavings and old cotton rugs and blankets usually serve very well.

The Stone-age Dog

A Spotted Dog from India, "Parent of the Modern Coach dog."

History of the Genus Canis

The history of man's association with the dog is a fascinating one, extending into the past at least seventy centuries, and involving the entire history of civilized man from the early Stone Age to the present.

The dog, technically a member of the genus *Canis,* belongs to the zoological family group *Canidae,* which also includes such animals as wolves, foxes, jackals, and coyotes. In the past it was generally agreed that the dog resulted from the crossing of various members of the family *Canidae.* Recent findings have amended this theory somewhat, and most authorities now feel the jackal probably has no direct relationship with the dog. Some believe dogs are descended from wolves and foxes, with the wolf the main progenitor. As evidence, they cite the fact that the teeth of the wolf are identical in every detail with those of the dog, whereas the teeth of the jackal are totally different.

Still other authorities insist that the dog always has existed as a separate and distinct animal. This group admits that it is possible for a dog to mate with a fox, coyote, or wolf, but points out that the resulting puppies are unable to breed with each other, although they can breed with stock of the same genus as either parent. Therefore, they insist, it was impossible for a new and distinct genus to have developed from such crossings. They then cite the fact that any dog can be mated with any other dog and the progeny bred among themselves. These researchers point out, too, heritable characteristics that are totally different in the three animals. For instance, the pupil of the dog's eye is round, that of the wolf oblique, and that of the jackal vertical. Tails, too, differ considerably, for tails of foxes, coyotes, and wolves always drop behind them, while those of dogs may be carried over the back or straight up.

Much conjecture centers on two wild dog species that still exist—the Dingo of Australia, and the Dhole in India. Similar in appearance, both are reddish in color, both have rather long,

slender jaws, both have rounded ears that stand straight up, and both species hunt in packs. Evidence indicates that they had the same ancestors. Yet, today, they live in areas that are more than 4,000 miles apart.

Despite the fact that it is impossible to determine just when the dog first appeared as a distinct species, archeologists have found definite proof that the dog was the first animal domesticated by man. When man lived by tracking, trapping, and killing game, the dog added to the forces through which man discovered and captured the quarry. Man shared his primitive living quarters with the dog, and the two together devoured the prey. Thus, each helped to sustain the life of the other. The dog assisted man, too, by defending the campsite against marauders. As man gradually became civilized, the dog's usefulness was extended to guarding the other animals man domesticated, and, even before the wheel was invented, the dog served as a beast of burden. In fact, archeological findings show that aboriginal peoples of Switzerland and Ireland used the dog for such purposes long before they learned to till the soil.

Cave drawings from the palaeolithic era, which was the earliest part of the Old World Stone Age, include hunting scenes in which a rough, canine-like form is shown alongside huntsmen. One of these drawings is believed to be 50,000 years old, and gives credence to the theory that all dogs are descended from a primitive type ancestor that was neither fox nor wolf.

Archeological findings show that Europeans of the New Stone Age possessed a breed of dogs of wolf-like appearance, and a similar breed has been traced through the successive Bronze Age and Iron Age. Accurate details are not available, though, as to the external appearance of domesticated dogs prior to historic times (roughly four to five thousand years ago).

Early records in Chaldean and Egyptian tombs show that several distinct and well-established dog types had been developed by about 3700 B.C. Similar records show that the early people of the Nile Valley regarded the dog as a god, often burying it as a mummy in special cemeteries and mourning its death.

Some of the early Egyptian dogs had been given names, such as Akna, Tarn, and Abu, and slender dogs of the Greyhound type and a short-legged Terrier type are depicted in drawings found

Bas-relief of Hunters with Nets and Mastiffs. From the walls of Assurbanipal's palace at Nineveh 668-626 B.C. *British Museum.*

in Egyptian royal tombs that are at least 5,000 years old. The Afghan Hound and the Saluki are shown in drawings of only slightly later times. Another type of ancient Egyptian dog was much heavier and more powerful, with short coat and massive head. These probably hunted by scent, as did still another type of Egyptian dog that had a thick furry coat, a tail curled almost flat over the back, and erect "prick" ears.

Early Romans and Greeks mentioned their dogs often in literature, and both made distinctions between those that hunted by sight and those that hunted by scent. The Romans' canine classifications were similar to those we use now. In addition to dogs comparable to the Greek sight and scent hounds, the ancient Romans had Canes *villatici* (housedogs) and Canes *pastorales* (sheepdogs), corresponding to our present-day working dogs.

The dog is mentioned many times in the Old Testament. The first reference, in Genesis, leads some Biblical scholars to assert that man and dog have been companions from the time man was created. And later Biblical references bring an awareness of the diversity in breeds and types existing thousands of years ago.

As civilization advanced, man found new uses for dogs. Some required great size and strength. Others needed less of these characteristics but greater agility and better sight. Still others needed an accentuated sense of smell. As time went on, men kept those puppies that suited specific purposes especially well and bred them together. Through ensuing generations of selective breeding, desirable characteristics appeared with increasing frequency. Dogs used in a particular region for a special purpose gradually became more like each other, yet less like dogs of other areas used for different purposes. Thus were established the foundations for the various breeds we have today.

The American Kennel Club, the leading dog organization in the United States, divides the various breeds into six "Groups," based on similarity of purposes for which they were developed.

"Sporting Dogs" include the Pointers, Setters, Spaniels, and Retrievers that were developed by sportsmen interested in hunting game birds. Most of the Pointers and Setters are of comparatively recent origin. Their development parallels the development of sporting firearms, and most of them evolved in the British Isles. Exceptions are the Weimaraner, which was developed in Ger-

many, and the Vizsla, or Hungarian Pointer, believed to have been developed by the Magyar hordes that swarmed over Central Europe a thousand years ago. The Irish were among the first to use Spaniels, though the name indicates that the original stock may have come from Spain. Two Sporting breeds, the American Water Spaniel, and the Chesapeake Bay Retriever, were developed entirely in the United States.

"Hounds," among which are Dachshunds, Beagles, Bassets, Harriers, and Foxhounds, are used singly, in pairs, or in packs to "course" (or run) and hunt for rabbits, foxes, and various rodents. But little larger, the Norwegian Elkhound is used in its native country to hunt big game—moose, bear, and deer.

The smaller Hound breeds hunt by scent, while the Irish Wolfhound, Borzoi, Scottish Deerhound, Saluki, and Greyhound hunt by sight. The Whippet, Saluki, and Greyhound are notably fleet of foot, and racing these breeds (particularly the Greyhound) is popular sport.

The Bloodhound is a member of the Hound Group that is known world-wide for its scenting ability. On the other hand, the Basenji is a comparatively rare Hound breed and has the distinction of being the only dog that cannot bark.

"Working Dogs" have the greatest utilitarian value of all modern dogs and contribute to man's welfare in diverse ways. The Boxer, Doberman Pinscher, Rottweiler, German Shepherd, Great Dane, and Giant Schnauzer are often trained to serve as sentries and aid police in patrolling streets. The German Shepherd is especially noted as a guide dog for the blind. The Collie, the various breeds of Sheepdogs, and the two Corgi breeds are known throughout the world for their extraordinary herding ability. And the exploits of the St. Bernard and Newfoundland are legendary, their records for saving lives unsurpassed.

The Siberian Husky and the Alaskan Malamute are noted for tremendous strength and stamina. Had it not been for these hardy Northern breeds, the great polar expeditions might never have taken place, for Admiral Byrd used these dogs to reach points inaccessible by other means. Even today, with our jet-age transportation, the Northern breeds provide a more practical means of travel in frigid areas than do modern machines.

"Terriers" derive their name from the Latin *terra,* meaning

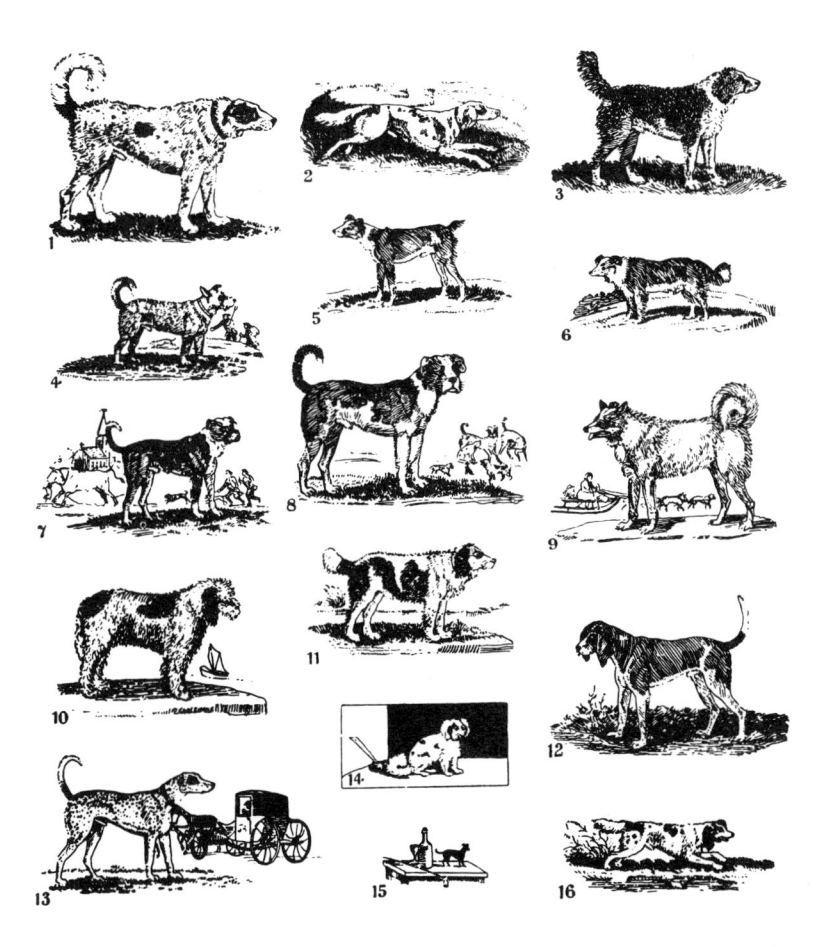

1. The Newfoundland. 2. The English Setter. 3. The Large Water-spaniel. 4. The Terrier. 5. The Cur-dog. 6. The Shepherd's Dog. 7. The Bulldog. 8. The Mastiff. 9. The Greenland Dog. 10. The Rought Water-dog. 11. The Small Water-spaniel. 12. The Old English Hound. 13. The Dalmatian or Coach-dog. 14. The Comporter (very much of a Papillon). 15. "Toy Dog, Bottle, Glass, and Pipe." *From a vignette.* 16. The Springer or Cocker. *From Thomas Bewick's "General History of Quadrupeds" (1790).*

"earth," for all of the breeds in this Group are fond of burrowing. Terriers hunt by digging into the earth to rout rodents and fur-bearing animals such as badgers, woodchucks, and otters. Some breeds are expected merely to force the animals from their dens in order that the hunter can complete the capture. Others are expected to find and destroy the prey, either on the surface or under the ground.

Terriers come in a wide variety of sizes, ranging from such large breeds as the Airedale and Kerry Blue to such small ones as the Skye, the Dandie Dinmont, the West Highland White, and the Scottish Terrier. England, Ireland, and Scotland produced most of the Terrier breeds, although the Miniature Schnauzer was developed in Germany.

"Toys," as the term indicates, are small breeds. Although they make little claim to usefulness other than as ideal housepets, Toy dogs develop as much protective instinct as do larger breeds and serve effectively in warning of the approach of strangers.

Origins of the Toys are varied. The Pekingese was developed as the royal dog of China more than two thousand years before the birth of Christ. The Chihuahua, smallest of the Toys, originated in Mexico and is believed to be a descendant of the Techichi, a dog of great religious significance to the Aztecs, while the Italian Greyhound was popular in the days of ancient Pompeii.

"Non-Sporting Dogs" include a number of popular breeds of varying ancestry. The Standard and Miniature Poodles were developed in France for the purpose of retrieving game from water. The Bulldog originated in Great Britain and was bred for the purpose of "baiting" bulls. The Chowchow apparently originated centuries ago in China, for it is pictured in a bas relief dated to the Han dynasty of about 150 B.C.

The Dalmatian served as a carriage dog in Dalmatia, protecting travelers in bandit-infested regions. The Keeshond, recognized as the national dog of Holland, is believed to have originated in the Arctic or possibly the Sub-Arctic. The Schipperke, sometimes erroneously described as a Dutch dog, originated in the Flemish provinces of Belgium. And the Lhasa Apso came from Tibet, where it is known as "Abso Seng Kye," the "Bark Lion Sentinel Dog."

During the thousands of years that man and dog have been closely associated, a strong affinity has been built up between the two. The dog has more than earned his way as a helper, and his faithful, selfless devotion to man is legendary. The ways in which the dog has proved his intelligence, his courage, and his dependability in situations of stress are amply recorded in the countless tales of canine heroism that highlight the pages of history, both past and present.

Dogs in Woodcuts. (*1st row*) (LEFT) "Maltese dog with shorter hair"; (RIGHT) "Spotted sporting dog trained to catch game"; (*2nd row*) (LEFT) Sporting white dog; (RIGHT) "Spanish dog with floppy ears": (*3rd row*) (LEFT) "French dog"; (RIGHT) "Mad dog of Grevinus"; (*4th row*) (LEFT) Hairy Maltese dog; (RIGHT) "English fighting dog ... of horrid aspect." *From Aldrovandus (1637).*

History of the English Springer Spaniel

The history of the English Springer Spaniel goes back several centuries to the time when hawking was the popular method of hunting game in England. Recorded history of the Springer starts about 1570 when Dr. Caius, a physician to Edward VI, used the term "springing spaniel" with reference to the land Spaniels used in the hawking of birds. The Spaniels "sprung" the birds—hence the term "springing spaniel," or "springer."

Later, when guns came into general use for the hunting of birds, the Spaniel was given a boost by Richard Surflet, a sportsman of the seventeenth century, who wrote that the Spaniel "is gentle loving and courteous to man more than any other dog. . . . of free untiring laborsome ranging, beating a full course over and over—which he does with a wanton playing taile and a busie labouring noise—neither desisting nor showing less delight in his labors at night than he did in the morning."

By 1800 there were three general classifications of Spaniels: the small ones, weighing up to twenty-five pounds and called "cockers" because they were used for hunting woodcock; the larger Spaniels, seventeen to eighteen inches tall and weighing twenty-five to forty-five pounds and simply called "field Spaniels"; and the third class, the English Spaniels assiduously bred in England. This class included the Springers, the Sussex Spaniels, and the Clumber Spaniels. The miniature or toy Spaniels fancied by King Charles and the Duke of Norfolk were called "comforts." This appellation referred to the fact that the small dogs were held in the lap for the purpose of providing warmth to their owners in the wintertime.

Several types of Spaniels were often whelped in the same litter, so the breed name applied to a particular dog was determined by his size and use rather than his bloodlines. Apparently, various types of Spaniels were interbred prior to the nineteenth century, without thought of standardization.

Beginning in 1813 the Boughey family of Aqualate in Shropshire, England, kept careful records of the breeding and whelping of a line of purebred Springer Spaniels. The Boughey family's studbook and whelping records were kept for approximately a century and consti-

Sire of Lubricant

Int. Ch. Belmon Countess, by Cocksure ex Flossie.

Ch. Belvidere Flossie and litter of puppies sired by Int. Ch. Inveresk Cocksure.

tute the oldest authentic records of Springer Spaniel bloodlines. The Bougheys attempted to produce dogs of uniform color, size, and hunting characteristics, and their breeding program left a permanent stamp on the breed.

It was about 1800 that Springers were first recorded as being used in America. At that time they were used to hunt the plentiful game in the eastern section of the United States, but by the time of the Civil War, the breed was receiving little attention and apparently had almost disappeared. But interest resurged in the eighties, and at the Madison Square Garden Show in 1886, a fair group of Springers was shown.

In 1900 the English were breeding for a large Spaniel (the Springer) and a small one (the Cocker). In 1902 the English Kennel Club recognized the English Springer Spaniel as a separate breed. With the consequent build-up in breeding in England, the Springer again came to the attention of American sportsmen, and in 1907 two English Springer Spaniels were brought to New Jersey by Robert D. Foster. However, no documented records of progeny can be found to validate these dogs as progenitors of the breed in America.

The first English Springer Spaniel to be registered in the United States was Denne Lucy, registered by The American Kennel Club in 1910. Unfortunately, the name of Lucy's owner is not available.

I hunted over an eighteen to nineteen inch all-liver dog in 1912, which was whelped of the union of two Cocker-size Spaniels—a cherry red sire and a black dam. The resulting litter of five had three Cocker-size bitches and two big Springer-size dogs. One was full bodied but short-legged. The other was a Springer from end to end, although he did not have a docked tail. But what a dog! He would hunt anything! And so I joined (or, rather, helped to lead) the legion of present-day "Springerites" who want to buy their children a Springer because they hunted over one years back.

Eventually, the Springer was brought from England to Canada, where interest immediately centered on the breed. C. E. Thomas of Victoria, British Columbia, owned the first Springer registered in Canada. This dog, Longbranch Teal, was registered in 1914. Eudore Chevrier kenneled Don Juan of Gerwyn, a sturdily built black and white dog, which had been brought to Winnipeg by W. H. Gardner after he purchased the dog at the Crufts Show in 1913. After trying Don Juan in the field, Mr. Chevrier purchased him as part of the foundation stock for his own Springer kennel. He also purchased two bitches imported from Beechgrove Kennels in England. Bred to Don Juan, the two produced puppies which were endorsed enthusiastically by Canadian sportsmen.

Freeman Lloyd of "Field and Stream" saw the Springers in action while judging a field trial in Canada. He became interested and told Mr. Chevrier there should be a good market for the breed in the United States. Acting on Mr. Lloyd's suggestion that he place an ad in "Field and Stream," Mr. Chevrier was unable to supply the resulting demand for puppies.

As an aftermath of World War I, Americans were highly sports-minded, and the new breed sounded exciting. Consequently, imports from England, not through Canada but directly to the United States, were soon the order of the day. Many new prefixes were established and Springers were in America to stay.

Under the impetus of the "roaring twenties," and the interest aroused by Freeman Lloyd's magazine articles, by "Gazette" articles, and by word of mouth, Springers rapidly gained a foothold in the United States. Production boomed in England as a result of the North American demand, and production in the United States soon began to expand.

By 1924 production was moving along well in both Canada and the United States and interest was high because most imports leaned heavily toward dual type—and most sportsmen were interested in the Springer as a hunting dog. Grouse, quail, woodcock, and ducks were plentiful and the Springer did a workmanlike job on them which thrilled the fancy tremendously. Then, through the efforts of Freeman Lloyd, the English Springer Spaniel Field Trial Association was formed in 1924. (This association is still recognized by The American Kennel Club as the parent club of the breed in the United States.) A Standard was written and was accepted and approved by The American Kennel Club.

Springers had been exhibited at various shows in the United States before 1920, but apparently it was at a show in Englewood, New Jersey, in 1923 that a class for Springers was first offered at an American show. Records for that period of time are meager and unfortunately do not include the name of the winner.

The first Springer to become a show champion in the United States was Ch. Horsford Highness, owned by Dr. A. C. Gifford, Oshkosh, Wisconsin. He acquired his title in 1923. The first Springer to become a field trial champion in the United States was Aughrim Flashing, bred by William Humphries of England. He was purchased by Mrs. Walter Ferguson, Jr., and acquired his title in 1929.

Beginning in the thirties, two bloodlines predominated in the eastern part of the United States—that of English Dual Ch. Horsford Hetman, bred by William Humphries in his Horsford Kennels in England, and that of United States Dual Ch. Tedwyn's Trex (1929), who was also an English field trial champion. The latter was owned by the legendary Ferguson family—Mr. and Mrs. Walter Ferguson, Jr., and Henry and Alfred Ferguson, whose efforts on behalf of the breed in the United States have often been compared with those of the Boughey family in England. The Fergusons gave unstintingly of their time, efforts, money, and extensive hospitality, and it was on the grounds of their estate on Fishers Island that the first Springer field trial in the United States was held in October 1924 by the English Springer Spaniel Field Trial Association.

Added to the bloodlines of Horsford Hetman and Tedwyn's Trex was that of another dog, English Ch. Rufton Recorder, who left an undying mark on the breed. Imported by Fred Hunt, Rufton Recorder won his American championship and sired thirty-one champions in this country, to take his place among the great sires of all breeds. He and his get appear in many Springer pedigrees today.

Mr. and Mrs. C. D. Jackson imported several top-flight show dogs to the West Coast, which laid a fine foundation for the breed out there, for that section of the country was more or less isolated from the rest of the country and Canada in those days.

In the mid-section of the country, the influx of imports from Canada helped set up many strains, and the pioneers of the breed did a terrific job and deserve much praise and our lasting thanks. Among those that promoted the breed were Dr. A. C. Gifford, Oshkosh, Wisconsin; Al Nichter, Canal Fulton, Ohio; Ed Knight, Charleston, West Virginia; and Fred Hunt, Green Valley Farm, Pennsylvania.

Int. Ch. Rufton Recorder

Ch. Inveresk Coronation

Ellwyn Countess

Springer whelped December 30, 1929, by Int. Ch. Inveresk Chancellor ex Int. Ch. Belmon Countess.

Imports and breeding caused the Springer to rise in one decade from the status of an almost unknown breed with only a handful of registrations to the breed ranking eighth numerically among all registered breeds. It would be of little value to enumerate here all the Springers imported to the United States during the twenties and thirties. Hundreds and hundreds were brought in from top-flight, well-known English kennels (and even some backyards). So bloodlines of American kennels soon overlapped.

Importation of bench dogs came to a virtual standstill in the United States in the forties, so 1942-43 marked the end of an era. At that time, many of the old-line breeders gave up. But as the old kennels closed, new ones opened.

Sandblown Acres was a new kennel which burst on the horizon. Owned by William Bellville, Sandblown Acres produced some of the most glamorous Springers in history. A combination of this line with the line of Ch. Showman of Shotton, one of the last great imports, produced American and Canadian Ch. Frejax Royal Salute, one of the all-time great winners. With a dog like Salute winning continuously in the greatest shows in the country, there ceased to be a good reason to import sires or dams of any type. American Springers had come of age—and many felt that we in this country could now breed the world's finest Springers.

Interest had simmered both on the bench and in the field from the twenties on into the fifties, and throughout this time there was a great deal of discussion regarding the merits of each of what had now become two types of Springers. Some stalwarts favored the field type, while other of the faithful favored a bench type. So sometimes it is hard to determine how the two types ever got off the same family tree under the same Standard. But field trial devotees run Springers in the field and bench addicts show their version of the Standard as bench dogs. This makes a nice arrangement for pet owners, for they can have one that looks like either of the two or a cross between— and they're happy, for they have a Springer.

In the last thirty years, imports have been limited and far less importance has been attached to those that have been brought in, for they have left less definite marks on the breed. Exports to England and other European countries have been made, and this fact definitely establishes the American type Springer as desirable. The headliner that started the trend was Ch. Timpanagos Adonis, who was shipped to Sweden, where he became both a bench and a field champion and was a boon to the Swedish breeding program.

Punch in the Garden.

Back Row: Ch. Belvidere Flossie, Triple Ch. Inveresk Collyshot, Int. Ch. Belmon Countess, Int. Ch. Inveresk Cocksure, and Ch. Inveresk Cuty. Front Row (puppies at six months): Belmon Abeline, Jacqueline, Prinsin, and Genteel.

Pillars of the Breed—1920 to 1970

In the first three decades of recent Springer history, from 1920 until 1950, there were many great dogs that enjoyed their place in the breed and passed on. But none made a record to surpass that made by Ch. Frejax Royal Salute, who was sired by Ch. Sir Lancelot of Salilyn and was out of Ch. Frejax Lilac Time. He represents the best of the intelligent breeding programs of two successful and famous kennels.

I was at the Westchester Show (then still on the golf-course site) when I saw the three "greats" of those days: Salute; the English Setter, Ch. Rock Falls Colonel; and the Boxer, Ch. Bang Away of Sirrah Crest. Three of the greatest of all time, these dogs rang up records as show winners in the mid-forties until the mid-fifties, with the famous English Setter, Ch. Man of Manidor, and the Smooth Fox Terrier, Ch. Nornay Saddler, giving them cause to try just a bit harder.

Salute's record as a sire, forty-four American champions out of twenty-six bitches, plus ten champions sired in Canada, is a record regarded for many years as being unbeatable—but records are made to be broken—and who knows when it may happen.

Salute, as number one Springer in America, was in great demand as a stud and his blood has infiltrated almost every strain of the breed in some way. He continued his reign into the fifties and while still in his prime underwent surgery performed by human brain surgeons in a big Detroit hospital. Unfortunately, he died, and the breed lost one of its greatest specimens. But he had laid the foundation for a type that varied from the earlier type—a rangier dog, but one still closely conforming to the Standard. We find that the color of the dogs became more normal, with liver and white, black and white, and tricolor predominating. There were no lemons, no oranges, and no off colors. Eyes darkened, haws were less noticeable, and many other faults prevalent in earlier years were bred out and disappeared.

In the forties and fifties, many new dogs forged to the front. Some of the greatest show dogs during this time were scattered about the country where they all made history: Ch. Audley Farm Judy, Ch. Rumak's King Cole, Ch. Runor's Agent, Ch. Runor's Deacon, Ch. Runor's Babette, Ch. Barrowdale's Flier, Ch. Barrowdale's Lady B, Ch. Cavalier of Caulier's, American and Canadian Ch. Covington

Inveresk Cashier

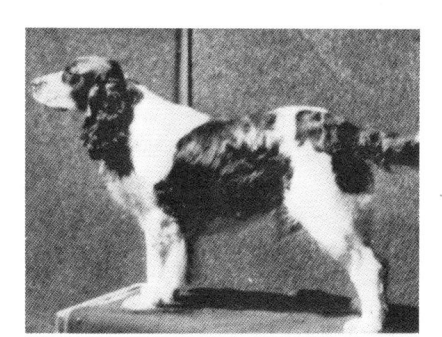

Int. Ch. Inveresk Clip

Int. Ch. Inveresk Comfort

Ellwyn Point

Imp. Rufton Ringleader

Int. Ch. Langtoon Lubricant

Free Lance Reporter, Ch. Eldgyth Adonis and Ch. Eldgyth Apollo, Ch. Maquam's Psalm Singer, Ch. Geiger's Chief Geronimo, American and Canadian Ch. Roger of Hunter's Hill, American and Canadian Ch. Melilotus Argonaut, Ch. Hillcrest Ginger Snap, Ch. Kelgate's Field Marshall, Ch. MacMar Pioneer, Ch. Millen Brae's Mr. McSniff, the forty champions of Melilotus, Ch. Wakefield's Black Knight, Ch. Wakefield's Fanny, Ch. Walpride Flaming Rocket (who sired forty-six or more champions), the fifty champions of Salilyn, the fifteen champions of Schwedekrest, Ch. Sunhi's Christmas Star, Ch. Syringa Sue, Ch. Tamridge Talisman, Ch. Timpanagos Mellinda, Ch. Waiterock's Elmer Brown (who sired forty champions in the Waiterock Kennels), and Ch. Kaintuck Christmas Star and the many champions bred in the Kaintuck Kennel.

These are a few of the great names that were making history and were cementing the foundations firmly for the fabulous sixties. The many owners whose kennels are not represented in the list should not feel slighted, for the few dogs named were but a part of the growth and building of the breed during the fifties. Many fine dogs played their part in the sixties and, consequently, belong to that era.

Through the years, Springers have made many outstanding show wins. In 1942, R. E. Allen's Ch. Timpanagos Melinda won the Group First at the Garden. Seven years later, Ch. Frejax Royal Salute repeated the win for Fred Jackson. And in 1955, Ch. King Peter of Salilyn took the award for Mrs. F. H. Gasow. And we were all very thrilled that Springers made these three wins out of fourteen years, with competition as it was then—tough.

In 1963, Group First went to Ch. Wakefield's Black Knight, and in 1967, Mrs. Gasow repeated the Group win with Ch. Salilyn's Aristocrat. In 1969, Wayne D. Magee's Ch. Magill's Patrick took the Group.

This made three times the breed won the Group in nine years. Incidentally, Mrs. F. H. Gasow's Salilyn Kennel produced two of the first six Group First winners. The 1963 winner, Ch. Wakefield's Black Knight went on to win Best in Show, the first Springer to have that honor.

1960 to 1970 was a great decade for the breed in that Springers won many of the largest shows in the country and were always a threat to contenders at all shows. In spite of terrific competition from other breeds, Springers held their own.

It looked as though the sixties were tops for the breed. Then along came February 16, 1971. A dog from Lexington, Kentucky, took the

Inveresk Connie

Ch. Inveresk Chancellor

Ch. Green Valley Elegance,
Ch. Green Valley Judy, and
Green Valley Punch.

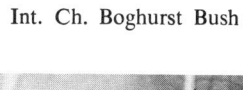

Int. Ch. Boghurst Bush

Breed, Group First, and the Show, for the second time for the breed. This dog, Ch. Chinoe's Adamant James, owned by Dr. Milton E. Prickett, was a son of Ch. Salilyn's Aristocrat ex Ch. Canarch Inchidony Brook. This handsome Springer had won at Philadelphia two months before and had started the year winning several Best-in-Show awards on the Florida circuit, winning the Garden, taking Best in Show at the International and at Harrisburg, Group First at Detroit, and Best in Show at Beverly Hills—and going like a ball of fire.

Adamant James went on to become the 1971 "Show Dog of the Year," with ninety-three Best-of-Breed, eighty-six Group First, and forty-eight Best-in-Show awards. Then he won the American Spaniel Show in January 1972 and repeated his Best-in-Show win at the Westminster Garden extravaganza in February. Since July 1, 1972, his showing has been very limited, but currently he is only a few hundred points off the top spot in the "Top Ten, Sporting" competition, and he is the only dog on the list with solid Group First awards.

Yes, Springers have come a long way. Many gallant dogs have been campaigned up and down the roads and have made names for themselves, their owners, and their breeders, and have gained the sobriquet of "Show Dog" from the fancy. Some have done so in spite of the fact that they were purchased as pets. For instance, Ch. Chinoe's Adamant James was a birthday gift to Dr. Prickett from his wife and family. Dr. Prickett had wanted a Springer to shoot over, having had one as a young man. So it goes—and the breeder sold another champion—which is even as you and I might have done.

But when one checks the lineage behind this great dog, it is obvious that he should be above average. A son of Ch. Salilyn's Aristocrat and Ch. Canarch Inchidony Brook is predestined to be endowed beyond the average.

If you really enjoy studying breeding, line breeding, inbreeding, and such, I suggest that you check the genealogical section of *The English Springer Spaniel in North America.* It is most interesting and informative—especially so for the sixties when dogs came forth at shows and won, finished their championships, and disappeared again. Others went on to produce get that won and finished as champions. They are the ones that will be in the second volume of the book.

Ch. Inveresk Carminetta

Green Valley Oak

Springer whelped December 6, 1929, by Int. Ch. Inveresk Chancellor ex Ch. Belmon Jacqueline.

Follow Through of Solway

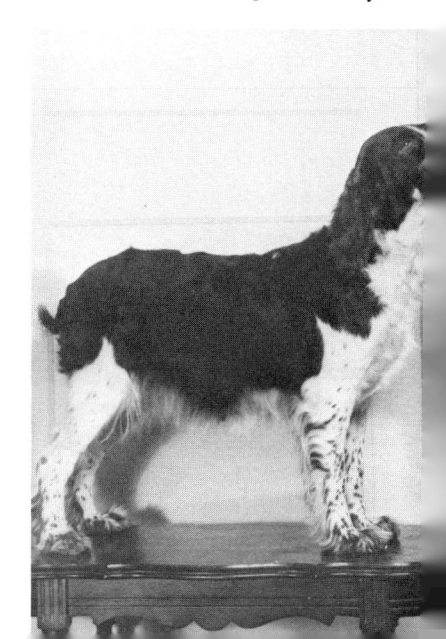

One of the curses of dog shows is the fact that so many fine dogs just wax on the vine—as a result of being campaigned to a championship and then pulled in and either forgotten or bred only to the owner's friends' inferior bitches. Thus, they complete an outstanding show career but never go on to contribute to the future of the breed.

One way to operate an unsuccessful kennel is to house inferior bitches and breed them to "one-shots," or similar quality dogs. Too many breeders forget that like begets like and that it is impossible to build on poor foundation stock. The great dogs of any breed are the results of intelligent breeding (not the catch as catch can type of breeding). When intelligent breeding programs are carried on long enough, new strains are added to the breed to replace old strains that are gradually lost because kennels eventually cease to function for one reason or another.

When we review the exploits of kennels that operated from the late fifties through the sixties, we find many interesting details. There were many new prefixes that took their places in the fold of dedicated Springer breeders, and some of those that started in the late fifties became full-fledged, leading strains in the sixties.

Though not complete, the following is a list of some of the kennels operated by dedicated breeders of the sixties that will probably continue to be well known among Springer breeders in the seventies: Adells, Andronicus, Anglodale Acres, Ascot, BeRay, Berclee, Beryltown, Canarch, Carey's, Cartref, Charlyte, Crooked Pine's, Elkgrove, Felicia, Footehill, Fortuna, Geiger, Green Pasture, Happy Hunting, Hillcrest, Huval, Inchidony, Kelgate, Kenlor, Lauranna, LeeVee's, Loresta, Loujon, MacMar, Marjon, Mullers, Pembroke, Return, Rexford, Richmond, Romig, Ruleon, Sandolyn, Schwedekrest, Shohunt, Skyline, Spring Hill, Syringa, Tamridge, Wakefield, Walpride, Wayside, and Welcome.

In the fifties and sixties we saw the rise and subsequent decline of many kennels. Among well-known kennels that went out of existence during the sixties are the following: Athadale, Audley Farm, Blairshinnoch, Bluestem, Bobbru, Boghurst, Breeze, Briarcliff, Caulier's, Donniedhu, Dormond, Earlsmoor, Eldgyth, Everrest, Frejax, Gay Beauties, Hampton, Kaintuck, Kay-Emm, Maquam, Melilotus, Pequa, Point Spa, Red Knob, Runor's, Skyline, South Riding, Timpanagos, and Willmar.

When one considers the number of Springer kennels operating in the United States, it almost seems there are enough to fill all requests for puppies from all over the country. But there is always a place for

Ch. Ebony of Hillcrest

additional dedicated breeders. Most of the top kennels that have closed down have done so as the result of extenuating circumstances, with the death of the kennel owner the chief cause—rather than loss of interest in the breed. Actually, we'll need many new breeders in the future and each year there are many breeders just getting their Springers started but capable of soaring to the heights if they maintain an even pace, have patience, and follow the basic precepts which have made this breed what it has become during its comparatively short sojourn in America.

In some respects it is unfortunate that our kennels are spread across such a vast area. If they were concentrated in a smaller area, various ideas of breeding and kenneling could be discussed. Such an arrangement would save a great deal of trouble, for there would be no purchasing sight unseen, no long distance shipping in order to breed animals, no arranging for breedings without looking first, as well as no guesswork.

For example, did you ever have a call regarding a breeding date, listen to the owner describe the bitch and give her pedigree, and then when she came you were shocked to see such a bitch? She was purebred—but how pure and what her sire and dam looked like are among the unanswerable questions.

In this country, there are strains developed that have no chance of being bettered in generations to come because there is no outcross available to bolster the line—that is, not the right one, the one that would do the line the most good. If a kennel has the advantage of housing many dogs—some straight line bred and some outcrosses—some experimental breeding can be done and the kennel can and often does produce good pups. But they are usually the result of the fact

that the bitch is so good that she can produce good progeny despite the fact that she is mated to a less than ideal stud dog. When a compatible breeding takes place—good bitch to good dog—a successful hit is usually made. If there are several good pups in the litter, it is worthwhile to plan future breedings to approximate the successful one insofar as strains are concerned.

Checking show results in the "Gazette" each month and writing a column have given me quite a knowledge of kennel prefixes, and judging and traveling over large sections of the country to judge have given me the opportunity for personal contact with many breeders, exhibitors, and handlers. These experiences have been both interesting and constructive. They have given me an inside look at a lot of the activities in the breed, and I have conversed with top breeders, who, for one reason or another have decided to get out of dogs.

I have also talked with old friends who have been on the verge for some time and are about to crash the gate to the inner sanctum. Champions will come more often to them, because they are better able to pick show prospects and because they concentrate on their breeding practices. Thus, their strain is in the final proving stage and the quality of their kennels is apparent and well recognized.

Back in the early fifties, while I was serving my apprenticeship, I acted as steward for a judge who, when he finished his stint in the ring, kindly offered to give me tips on judging Springers. So we went to a ring where Springers were to be judged and my friend asked the officiating judge to gait the dogs from our corner. The judge did so, and my friend carefully criticized twenty-seven Springers for my edification. I owe him a deep debt of gratitude. To this day I can hear his quiet voice describing those dogs—their good and bad qualities, and the kennel or family strain from which most of them came.

In those earlier years, I heard many judges say that they could spot the dogs of certain kennels when they saw them in a ring. Well, I haven't heard such comments in recent years, for the top strains and kennels have so many good dogs that it is impossible to figure pedigrees as was done years ago.

But there still remain some distinct features among Springers across the country. Because the country is so large, there are differences in dogs. Still, most breeders have mental pictures of Springers that are very much alike. But living conditions, characteristics of top stock, weather conditions, and other factors do cause differences among dogs.

Ch. Kaintuck Tolstoy, by Ch. Charlyle's Fair Warning ex Ch. Kaintuck Fortune Huntress. Breeder, Stuart H. Johnson. Owner, Dana Hopkins.

Top Kennels in the United States

Although I have visited many of the fine kennels in America, I am sorry to say that I have missed many I would have liked to visit. There is not space here to describe all I've visited, so I'll just mention some of the largest and some of the smallest—but all among the most successful.

I made several visits to Melilotus, Salilyn, Maquam, Ascot, Hillcrest, Charlyle, Kelgate, Willmar, Blairshinnoch, Romig's, Wakefield, Point Spa, Bobbru, Eldgyth, and Walpride—just to name a few—where puppies were delightful and old pensioners brought tears to the eyes as they asked for the top place just once more. Champions were haughty and near-champions were beginning to get that way, and the brood bitches just said "hello" and went on about their daily lives.

At Melilotus, I saw many of the great ones, including Amos, Tranquility, Royal Oak, and others—high on a hill at Bethel, in an old apple orchard where they could loll at ease and spend their days in peace. I remember eating big cold strawberries with cream and sugar in Revere bowls one Sunday morning at Melilotus. Everything on the table that could be was made of silver and all had been won by the dogs of Melilotus. The breakfast that Sunday was my last at Melilotus—up on that high hill in Connecticut where the genial R. Gilman Smith was host and his gracious lady, Bea, was most considerate of all who were present.

At Salilyn, with penful after penful of dogs of all ages, just to start thinking of how many champions came out of that whelping house made one ponder on the works of the Almighty. It just didn't seem possible for humans alone to do such a job. And such dogs—tails wagging, each one waiting for the hands that govern Salilyn.

Maquam, where dogs were in the kennel, the house, and the yard, the grande dame, Lady Marguerite, loved them all. And only she could keep them straight as they milled about the rambling house, barn, and grounds.

Ascot started in 1955 at a beautiful New England farm outside Hartford, Connecticut, in a renovated barn with all modern kennel improvements. The foundation stock was from Runor with Melilotus added. Fifteen or more bench champions were bred at Ascot, and the

Ch. Return Remembrance, winning Best of Opposite Sex at 1963 American Spaniel Club Show.

Ch. Salilyn's Aristocrat, winning First in the Sporting Group at the 1967 Heart of America Kennel Club Show.

Ascot strain has been inculcated into many other kennels, with fine results adding to the glory of the breed.

At Hillcrest in Wisconsin, Henrietta Schmidt heads a dynasty with champions since 1959. The kennels were the pride and joy of the late Henry Phillips and his wife of Elkhorn, Wisconsin, but are now given over to Henrietta to manage.

Charlyle, owned by Charles and the late Lyle Clements in Milwaukee, is the home of many champions. With kennel quarters about the size of four phone booths and a fifteen foot square yard under a big tree, Charlyle has Springer fever all over the place. Charlie Clements is in his eighties but is still tough competition. He united efforts with Anne Pope several years ago, and she campaigned Charlyle's Fair Warning through the Midwest and the East to set both an impressive show record and an impressive record as a sire. Charlyle's first champion was a blue roan import—Merely Jerry. The kennel is a fantastic one, but periodically brings forth another champion in spite of being limited by local ordinances to no more than two adult Springers at one time. So it does take about three years to get another champion—which is worth a handclap, for it has been done regularly. There are plenty of breeders who agree to disagree with Charlie and who are producing good dogs because of it and because of him.

Kelgate, established in Ithaca, New York, in 1951 by Emmy Fagan, was moved to Leroy, Ohio, a few years ago. There the kennel owners hope to add more names to the list of champions carrying the Kelgate prefix. Their bench dogs are bred for soundness and quality.

Willmar Kennel was owned by the late William and Margaret Johnson, who started breeding in 1942. Both passed away in 1962. The foundation stock was Ch. Rivercrest Whirlaway, bred by John Dietz of Wisconsin, and Belfield Evening Star, bred by Dr. Harry Steinbach, Ambler, Pennsylvania. Willmar bred five champions, and one, Ch. Willmar's Whirlaway, owned by Mrs. Barthell of Norristown, Pennsylvania, won Best of Breed at Westminster in 1953.

Blairshinnoch was established by Jim Forbes twenty years ago and with Ch. Barrowdale's Lady B as foundation bitch, soon was on its way. A dual type Springer, Lady B earned a working certificate at age ten and was still going strong in the field several years later. Only death ended her hunting and showing. But her son, John O'Groats, lived on to head the kennel until it was given up and the Forbeses retired.

Romig's Kennel is in Pennsylvania, where Hazel Romig has bred and owned Springers since the forties. Hazel Romig is a charter mem-

Ch. Marjon's Sweet Cassia going Best of Winners and Winners Bitch at 1971 National Specialty Show. Judge, Clifton C. Hulsey. Handler, Vern Johnson. Owners, Peggy and Vern Johnson.

Viking Eric of Lleda, winning the Group at 1968 Bronx County Kennel Club Match Show.

ber of the Keystone English Springer Spaniel Club—the only charter member left in the club—and one of its hardest working members. She was the breeder of my first Springer, Romig's Chocolate Prince. A tough competitor, this Springer gal was more thrilled than I can say when Ch. Willmar's Maggie was top winner at Trenton years ago. (And, incidentally, she is a good loser, too.)

Wakefield Kennel was the home of the immortal Ch. Wakefield's Black Knight, the first Springer to take Westminster Best in Show, and the one that put Springers on an everlasting pedestal in dog history. Wakefield is a small, neat, but handy kennel, where champions are made nearly every year. It has a long line of winners with most of the sixteen to eighteen champions sired by Black Knight or out of Ch. Wakefield's Fanny, his dam. Most kennels in the East have Wakefield blood in their lines. The breed is a better one, thanks to the ever gracious mistress of this kennel and her love of Springers.

Point Spa Kennel, now closed, is another in the East that I have known and that I watched develop and succeed. Fifteen champions all went down to the same bloodline from Pola, the foundation bitch at Point Spa. Every Point Spa bench champion was hunted and shot over before being shown—so show dogs *can* be shot over and gun dogs *can* be shown. This kennel strain has been saved by Ch. Point Spa Gay Star's going to live at Spring Hill, where Hubert and Elizabeth Schwerdie hold forth—and have a number of champions which they show throughout the East.

Bobbru Kennels, high on a hill near Lambertville, New Jersey, was owned by the Patons. This kennel was the home of Ch. Skyline Fast and foundation bitch Ch. Rosemary of Melilotus, both by Ch. Amos of Melilotus. It had eight champions and all pups were field and bench trained. A number of fine gun dogs carried this prefix.

Eldgyth was the prefix of John M. Freeman, who last lived near Norristown and had his Springer kennel from 1935 to 1958. His two Apollo dogs took both A.S.C. and Westminster Shows and had a wonderful run of wins on their records.

Walpride has a definite thirty-year strain in its kennel in Clarence, New York (outside of Buffalo), where Robert and Leona Walgate have bred the outstanding dogs they have shown in Canada and all points in the northeastern section of the United States. Walpride has had more than forty champions in thirty years, and all its dogs are bred for show, hunting, and companionship. American and Canadian Ch. Walpride's Sandman took Best in Show in six Canadian shows. American and Canadian Ch. Walpride's Flaming Rocket sired more

Ch. Marjon's Sparkling Charger

Ch. Scotch Mist of Pequa

Ch. Charlyle's Fair Warning

than forty champion get and is probably one of the greatest Springer sires of all time.

Yes, I was lucky to be alive during these great years of the forties, fifties, and sixties—lucky to be able to visit just these few kennels out of the many scattered across the country. It gave me an inside look at a great number of dogs that went on to win and put their names among the greats of the breed.

Such dogs as were those in the few kennels discussed! And to think of all the other great ones—Springers all—that were whelped and lived elsewhere, in large kennels or small, everywhere in this great country. Their names are there, too, among the stars. And they, too, made history, because they, too, were Springers.

Kennels in the East include Tamridge, owned by Charles and Barbara Parker, where all dogs are field trained and show trained, to possess in the ring "the tireless, eager ability in the field that we like" —so says the mistress of Tamridge. And their linebred entries hold their own at most Eastern shows.

Runor's Kennel, a name known wherever there are Springers, started in 1937 with Audley Farm Judy (dam of twelve champions) as foundation bitch. About twenty champions carry the Runor's prefix and the strain and blood are in many lines throughout Springerdom. Runor's Kennel started as an off-shoot of the Audley Farm Kennel owned by the late Robert Morrow, older brother of the late T. Norman Morrow, who owned Runor's Kennel. Both kennels bred dual purpose dogs, and, fortunately, the knowledge of these two men regarding Springers has been passed on to many breeders.

Pequa Kennels was a force in the East for many years, and there Albert and Elsie Matson and their family held forth—breeding, whelping, training, handling, and talking Springers at every show within miles of Long Island. Pequa operated for about twenty years, until death stepped in and both Albert and Elsie passed away. After severe attacks of arthritis, Elsie consistently attended shows throughout the East in a wheel chair, but she got there, along with each new dog and each new grandchild.

Return, another dual type kennel, is owned by William and Jesse Gebert, whose goal is "good hunters which can be winners in the show ring." Most of Return's champions carry Winners Certificates and they are in most rings in the East facing all competition.

James and Dorothy Fortuna have finished several bench champions and love their black and whites. Since 1953 they have been most constant in attendance at all the big shows in the East and have finished

eight or nine champions. Ch. Syringa Sue was a foundation bitch, which gave them a Runor and Melilotus foundation to build on.

Kaintuck's breeding started in 1950 and ended in 1968 with the owner's death. A kennel of great dogs, Kaintuck had a line of black and white Springers that was known internationally, for there were several Specialty Shows held in the East where all top awards went to Kaintuck dogs. Ch. Kaintuck Christmas Carol sired Ch. Wakefield's Black Knight and many other fine dogs.

Shohunt Springers and the Klembaras with lunch, a corn roast, or something, made a show official. The good Doctor goes way back in the breed to when "Hector was a Pup."

Montour Kennels, Pittsburgh, Pennsylvania, was owned by the late Miss Mary McCune, who campaigned black and white dogs. She had the late Harold Correll, a professional handler, get together for her kennel top Springers from Runor, Point Spa, Charlyle, and Covington. American and Canadian Ch. Covington Free Lance Reporter was top dog, winning the breed at the Garden, the International in Chicago, and Morris & Essex, as well as many other shows.

Rodleigh, owned by Roger and Lee Batchelder, was formerly in Weston, Connecticut. These two most hardy members of the Eastern Springer Spaniel Club moved their dogs and kennel to Arizona, where they built a new home and kennel and are now attending shows in that section of the country as well as Southern California.

Berclee, a small kennel run by two nice ladies in the Washington area, without fancy kenneling facilities, has quality not quantity. Berclee has something good in nearly every show of distinction in the East.

Beryltown Kennel has had a most successful breeding program with its foundation bitch, Ch. Cartref Donla's Arpege, the dam of eight or more champions. Most Beryltown Springers are obedience trained and all are dogs of fine disposition and a credit to the breed.

Carey's—the kennel of Andrew and Mary Carey—is breeding not only for dual contenders but also for triple. All dogs shown are worked under guns and taught obedience. They must have obedience degrees, Winners Certificates, and points in the show ring. Carey's is a definite strain of well-behaved, obedient, and fun-loving Springers.

Getting back into the Midwest—in addition to the kennels on which I've already commented, there is another which I have always wanted to visit. It is the kennel first owned by W. E. MacKinney, where there are more English imports today than in any other kennel I know about in this country. Mac has long been an exponent of "hunting show

dogs" and since I saw one of his dogs worked in the rain in an open field at the Keystone National Springer Specialty, I have had a terrific yen to watch more MacMar show dogs in the field.

Crooked Pine's at Ingleside, Illinois, is owned by Joan Ross, who had Ch. King William of Salilyn—a good stud and one that made a fine record as such while living under the Crooked Pine's banner. His son, Ch. Crooked Pine's Burgoo Boy, sired many champions. Bitches from this kennel have always been top competition.

Conarch Kennels, owned by Charles and Mary Lee Hendee, Farmington, Michigan, had as its foundation bitch Melilotus Hufty Tufty, by the English import, Ch. Rosthorne Hunter. Hufty's daughter, Canarch Sunnyside, was Canarch's first champion.

Gay Beauties Kennel, owned by Thomas A. Blessing, Grosse Point, Michigan, finished a dozen champions. Ch. Gay Beauties Academy Award was credited with ten of them.

Inchidony is owned by Mr. and Mrs. Becher Hungerford—and what a couple of eras they have had, with two top ones—one liver and white and the other black and white—taking "the marbles" in the East and Midwest constantly. Both prepotent sires, these two established two strains from Ch. Inchidony Prince Charming—that of the Salilyn Kennel and that of Charlyle—that will stay with Springers for years to come. These two sires can take all top awards at shows, with their get taking Winners Dog, Winners Bitch, Best of Winners, and Best of Opposite Sex—after 'daddy" takes Best of Breed. Yes, Ch. Salilyn's Aristocrat and Ch. Charlyle's Fair Warning have made exceptional Records.

Unfortunately, the great sire, Ch. Inchidony Prince Charming, died in June 1972. But his record as a sire is one of the greatest of all time.

Loujon, New Richmond, Ohio, is owned by John and Louise Greeno, who started with Ch. Cartref Moonwink. Breeders of several fine champions, they support bench showing, obedience, field trials, and working tests.

In the Southwest, the Tri Trump Kennels of Helen Tindall, San Antonio, Texas, bred bench champions and many fine dogs. The foundation bitch was of Kesterson background.

LeeVee's, owned by Lee and Vivian Diefendaffer, developed a strain worked down from Ch. LeeVee's High Trump (sire of more than fifty champions). Another great sire at LeeVee's, Ch. Debonair Dandy, was out of Ch. LeeVee's High Trump and Ch. My Fair Julie.

In the West, at Barblythe in Beverly Hills, the O. H. Parkenings

Ch. Blairshinnoch John O'Groats

and daughter Lucille bred a dozen or more champions of lines dominated by Ch. Showman of Shotton, together with sons Ch. Roger of Hunter's Hill, Ch. Timpanagos Radar, and Ch. Show King of Boghurst.

Breeze, at Edgewater, Colorado, owned by Betty Buchanan, started in 1925 with a blue roan, Flint's Whimsey, a son of Vivandiere of Avandale and Ch. Flint of Avandale. This kennel bred the famous Ch. Woodelf of Breeze, who later was leased to Green Valley Kennels and bred to Ch. Rufton Recorder, with this first litter going to Green Valley, and, bred her next season, with this second litter to be owned by Breeze. The first litter made history. It consisted of seven pups—six which became champions and the unshown Orentia. The latter, as a brood bitch, put her long-time record in the books to far outshine her champion sisters and brothers. The second litter produced two champions—giving the dam eight champions, which was a record for years. Now, after twenty years, this strain of Springers constitutes the principal background bloodline of most American bench champions. It produced seventy-two champions, including one dual champion. Fred Hunt, the owner of Green Valley Kennel, made a great contribution when he imported Rufton-bred dogs and field trial bitches and kept the blood of dogs of hunting instinct in his lines and his strain. A complete book could be written on the impact this kennel has had on the breed in America—and will have for years to come.

Hunter's Hill Kennel was started by Dorothy B. Klokke of Pasadena, California, after she imported Ch. Rufton Pattern to this coun-

try. Breeding to Ch. Showman of Shotton produced seven champions in two litters. One of these champions, Roger of Hunter's Hill, sired twenty-two champions, one of which was Ch. Melilotus Argonaut, who sired seventeen. Hunter's Hill established a definite strain that did a great deal for Springers on the West Coast. Mrs. Klokke is recognized as one of the long-time and outstanding breeders of Springers and one of the breed's staunchest advocates. Her ideas and ideals have helped the breed tremendously.

Kay-Emm Kennels, owned by Mr. and Mrs. K. M. McDonald in Redondo Beach, California, was started with Boghurst-Hunter's Hill stock. The McDonalds finished eight or more champions.

Kenlor is another California kennel which came to the fore in the fifties. It was owned by Lorraine and the late Kenneth Hayes, who set up shop with a pup from a Timpanagos dog and a Hunter's Hill bitch. They bred hunting-show dogs and made eight or more champions. Lorraine suffered severely when Kenneth passed away but is gallantly carrying on and the kennel is still going strong.

Loresta, at Fontana, California, is owned by Ed and Lillian Stapp. Ch. Gay Princess Cocoa is matron of the kennel, they tell me. Kennel runs go right to the rear door of the house and every dog shares in the family life. Consequently, the dogs have good dispositions. The kennel has produced seven champions from litters out of Gay Princess.

Millen Brae, Kansas City, Missouri, is owned by Roy McMillan, who has owned Springers for over thirty years. He has bred five champions, including the outstanding Ch. Millen Brae's Mr. McSniff, a Best-in-Show winner. This kennel breeds dual-type Springers (field trial and bench), and shows sparingly but always wins.

Waiterock, in Lafayette, California, began with all western-bred foundation stock which had been bred for dual characteristics. Pups are usually gun and obedience trained before being sold. Outcrosses have been made to bring in desired characteristics, and more than forty bench champions have been credited to the prefix. The greatest, American and Canadian Ch. Waiterock's Elmer Brown, was homebred and was one of the all-time greats in American show annals. He could move with the peers among sporting dogs, including all breeds in the Group. This kennel has established its own strain and could go on for years within its own kennel limits, for breeding here is a fetish and correct breeding practices are adhered to assiduously by both owners—Bert and Juanita Waite Howard.

Marjon, in Orange, California, was started by Vern and Peggy Johnson with Hunter's Hill foundation stock and has bred some nice

Ch. Marjon's Licorice Twist, Best of Breed at Kennel Club of Pasadena Show in 1971. Handler, Corky Vroom. Owners, Peggy and Vern Johnson.

champions in the past years. This kennel can go on to fill in for and to take the place of California kennels of long standing that have discontinued breeding for one reason or another. The Johnsons started in 1959 and have held the banner high for Springers ever since, producing new champions regularly.

In the Northwest is Schwedekrest, in Washington State. Louise Schwede runs this kennel, the home of fifteen or more champions, and carries the banner very high when it comes to proclaiming Springers as being a breed to dream with. She has built the kennel with Ch. Melilotus Little Acorn as foundation sire and three bitches—all of which were descendants of Ch. Tranquility of Melilotus—as foundation bitches. Tranquility was Best of Opposite Sex to the Springer of the Year for three different years. Schwedekrest, an offshoot of Melilotus, clear across the country, is doing a job—and a good one.

Geiger Kennels of North Bend, Washington, owned by Mr. and Mrs. Robert Geiger, breed bench dogs that are obedience trained and shot over. The foundation bitch is Ch. Schwedekrest Lady Pamela. The Geigers have produced six champions.

During the past half century of Springer activity in the United States, such greats as Eudore Chevrier, Freeman Lloyd, Herbert Routley, Henry Ferguson, Ed Knight, Dr. A. C. Gifford, Dr. Samuel Milbank, Joseph Quirk, Arthur Caulier, Bob and Norm Morrow, William Elder, Kenny Hayes, and many others, did much to promote the breed. In the foregoing pages, many of the important American breeders, owners, kennels and dogs have been discussed. There are many others that merit discussion, but, unfortunately, lack of space makes it impossible to include them here.

In Canada, there are many Springer kennels, but I am familiar only with the few that show in this country. Among them are the kennels of Lillah Lymburner and Anne Snelling. Both ladies have shown dogs in the United States and belong to the Eastern English Springer Spaniel Club.

Mr. and Mrs. Lymburner bred American and Canadian Ch. Covington Free Lance Reporter and later sold him to Miss Mary McCune of Pittsburgh. Campaigned by Harold Correll, this Springer won many Groups as well as Best-of-Breed placings in shows in all sections of the Midwest and the East.

Mrs. Anne Snelling has many fine dogs in her Oaktree Kennels in Ottawa, and her American and Canadian Ch. Oaktree Lancashire Poacher, handled exclusively by William Trainor, has done some fine winning at New England and Eastern shows in the past few years.

Ch. Lleda's Springhill April Fool

Manners for the Family Dog

Although each dog has personality quirks and idiosyncrasies that set him apart as an individual, dogs in general have two characteristics that can be utilized to advantage in training. The first is the dog's strong desire to please, which has been built up through centuries of association with man. The second lies in the innate quality of the dog's mentality. It has been proved conclusively that while dogs have reasoning power, their learning ability is based on a direct association of cause and effect, so that they willingly repeat acts that bring pleasant results and discontinue acts that bring unpleasant results. Hence, to take fullest advantage of a dog's abilities, the trainer must make sure the dog understands a command, and then reward him when he obeys and correct him when he does wrong.

Commands should be as short as possible and should be repeated in the same way, day after day. Saying "Heel," one day, and "Come here and heel," the next will confuse the dog. *Heel, sit, stand, stay, down,* and *come* are standard terminology, and are preferable for a dog that may later be given advanced training.

Tone of voice is important, too. For instance, a coaxing tone helps cajole a young puppy into trying something new. Once an exercise is mastered, commands given in a firm, matter-of-fact voice give the dog confidence in his own ability. Praise, expressed in an exuberant tone will tell the dog quite clearly that he has earned his master's approval. On the other hand, a firm "No" indicates with equal clarity that he has done wrong.

Rewards for good performance may consist simply of praising lavishly and petting the dog, although many professional trainers use bits of food as rewards. Tidbits are effective only if the dog is hungry, of course. And if you smoke, you must be sure to wash your hands before each training session, for the odor of nicotine is repulsive to dogs. On the hands of a heavy smoker, the odor of nicotine may be so strong that the dog is unable to smell the tidbit.

Correction for wrong-doing should be limited to repeating "No," in a scolding tone of voice or to confining the dog to his bed. Spanking or striking the dog is taboo—particularly using sticks, which might cause injury, but the hand should never be used either. For field training as well as some obedience work, the hand is used to signal the dog. Dogs that have been punished by slapping have a tendency to cringe whenever they see a hand raised and consequently do not respond promptly when the owner's intent is not to punish but to signal.

Some trainers recommend correcting the dog by whacking him with a rolled-up newspaper. The idea is that the newspaper will not injure the dog but that the resulting noise will condition the dog to avoid repeating the act that seemingly caused the noise. Many authorities object to this type of correction, for it may result in the dog's becoming "noise-shy"—a decided disadvantage with show dogs which must maintain poise in adverse, often noisy, situations. "Noise-shyness" is also an unfortunate reaction in field dogs, since it may lead to gun-shyness.

To be effective, correction must be administered immediately, so that in the dog's mind there is a direct connection between his act and the correction. You can make voice corrections under almost any circumstances, but you must never call the dog to you and then correct him, or he will associate the correction with the fact that he has come and will become reluctant to respond. If the dog is at a distance and doing something he shouldn't, go to him and scold him while he is still involved in wrong-doing. If this is impossible, ignore the offense until he repeats it and you can correct him properly.

Especially while a dog is young, he should be watched closely and stopped before he gets into mischief. All dogs need to do a certain amount of chewing, so to prevent your puppy's chewing something you value, provide him with his own rubber balls and toys. Never allow him to chew cast-off slippers and then expect him to differentiate between cast-off items and those you value. Nylon stockings, wooden articles, and various other items may cause intestinal obstructions if the dog chews and swallows them, and death may result. So it is essential that the dog be permitted to chew only on bones or rubber toys.

Serious training for obedience should not be started until a

dog is a year old. But basic training in house manners should begin the day the puppy enters his new home. A puppy should never be given the run of the house but should be confined to a box or small pen except for play periods when you can devote full attention to him. The first thing to teach the dog is his name, so that whenever he hears it, he will immediately come to attention. Whenever you are near his box, talk to him, using his name repeatedly. During play periods, talk to him, pet him, and handle him, for he must be conditioned so he will not object to being handled by a veterinarian, show judge, or family friend. As the dog investigates his surroundings, watch him carefully and if he tries something he shouldn't, reprimand him with a scolding "No!" If he repeats the offense, scold him and confine him to his box, then praise him. Discipline must be prompt, consistent, and always followed with praise. Never tease the dog, and never allow others to do so. Kindness and understanding are essential to a pleasant, mutually rewarding relationship.

When the puppy is two to three months old, secure a flat, narrow leather collar and have him start wearing it (never use a harness, which will encourage tugging and pulling). After a week or so, attach a light leather lead to the collar during play sessions and let the puppy walk around, dragging the lead behind him. Then start holding the end of the lead and coaxing the puppy to come to you. He will then be fully accustomed to collar and lead when you start taking him outside while he is being housebroken.

Housebreaking can be accomplished in a matter of approximately two weeks provided you wait until the dog is mature enough to have some control over bodily functions. This is usually at about four months. Until that time, the puppy should spend most of his day confined to his penned area, with the floor covered with several thicknesses of newspapers so that he may relieve himself when necessary without damage to floors.

Either of two methods works well in housebreaking—the choice depending upon where you live. If you live in a house with a readily accessible yard, you will probably want to train the puppy from the beginning to go outdoors. If you live in an apartment without easy access to a yard, you may decide to train him first to relieve himself on newspapers and then when he

has learned control, to teach the puppy to go outdoors.

If you decide to train the puppy by taking him outdoors, arrange some means of confining him indoors where you can watch him closely—in a small penned area, or tied to a short lead (five or six feet). Dogs are naturally clean animals, reluctant to soil their quarters, and confining the puppy to a limited area will encourage him to avoid making a mess.

A young puppy must be taken out often, so watch your puppy closely and if he indicates he is about to relieve himself, take him out at once. If he has an accident, scold him and take him out so he will associate the act of going outside with the need to relieve himself. Always take the puppy out within an hour after meals—preferably to the same place each time—and make sure he relieves himself before you return him to the house. Restrict his water for two hours before bedtime and take him out just before you retire for the night. Then, as soon as you wake in the morning, take him out again.

For paper training, set aside a particular room and cover a large area of the floor with several thicknesses of newspapers. Confine the dog on a short leash and each time he relieves himself, remove the soiled papers and replace them with clean ones.

As his control increases, gradually decrease the paper area, leaving part of the floor bare. If he uses the bare floor, scold him mildly and put him on the papers, letting him know that there is where he is to relieve himself. As he comes to understand the idea, increase the bare area until papers cover only space equal to approximately two full newspaper sheets. Keep him using the papers, but begin taking him on a leash to the street at the times of day that he habitually relieves himself. Watch him closely when he is indoors and at the first sign that he needs to go, take him outdoors. Restrict his water for two hours before bedtime, but if necessary, permit him to use the papers before you retire for the night.

Using either method, the puppy will be housebroken in an amazingly short time. Once he has learned control he will need to relieve himself only four or five times a day.

Informal obedience training, started at the age of about six to eight months, will provide a good background for any advanced training you may decide to give your dog later. The collar most

effective for training is the metal chain-link variety. The correct size for your dog will be about one inch longer than the measurement around the largest part of his head. The chain must be slipped through one of the rings so the collar forms a loop. The collar should be put on with the loose ring at the right of the dog's neck, the chain attached to it coming over the neck and through the holding ring, rather than under the neck. Since the dog is to be at your left during most of the training, this makes the collar most effective.

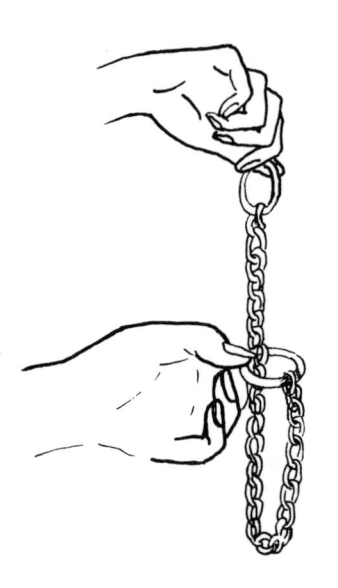

The leash should be attached to the loose ring, and should be either webbing or leather, six feet long and a half inch to a full inch wide. When you want your dog's attention, or wish to correct him, give a light, quick pull on the leash, which will momentarily tighten the collar about the neck. Release the pressure instantly, and the correction will have been made. If the puppy is already accustomed to a leather collar, he will adjust easily to the training collar. But before you start training sessions, practice walking with the dog until he responds readily when you increase tension on the leash.

Set aside a period of fifteen minutes, once or twice a day, for regular training sessions, and train in a place where there will be no distractions. Teach only one exercise at a time, making

sure the dog has mastered it before going on to another. It will probably take at least a week for the dog to master each exercise. As training progresses, start each session by reviewing exercises the dog has already learned, then go on to the new exercise for a period of concerted practice. When discipline is required, make the correction immediately, and always praise the dog after corrections as well as when he obeys promptly. During each session stick strictly to business. Afterwards, take time to play with the dog.

The first exercise to teach is heeling. Have the dog at your left and hold the leash as shown in the illustration on the preceding page. Start walking, and just as you put your foot forward for the first step, say your dog's name to get his attention, followed by the command, "Heel!" Simultaneously, pull on the leash lightly. As you walk, try to keep the dog at your left side, with his head alongside your left leg. Pull on the leash as necessary to urge him forward or back, to right or left, but keep him in position. Each time you pull on the leash, say "Heel!" and praise the dog lavishly. When the dog heels properly in a straight line, start making circles, turning corners, etc.

Once the dog has learned to heel well, start teaching the "sit." Each time you stop while heeling, command "Sit!" The dog will be at your left, so use your left hand to press on his rear and guide him to a sitting position, while you use the leash in your right hand to keep his head up. Hold him in position for a few moments while you praise him, then give the command to heel. Walk a few steps, stop, and repeat the procedure. Before long he will automatically sit whenever you stop. You can then teach the dog to "sit" from any position.

When the dog will sit on command without correction, he is ready to learn to stay until you release him. Simply sit him, command "Stay!" and hold him in position for perhaps half a minute, repeating "Stay," if he attempts to stand. You can release him by saying "O.K." Gradually increase the time until he will stay on command for three or four minutes.

The "stand-stay" should also be taught when the dog is on leash. While you are heeling, stop and give the command "Stand!" Keep the dog from sitting by quickly placing your left arm under him, immediately in front of his right hind leg. If he

continues to try to sit, don't scold him but start up again with the heel command, walk a few steps, and stop again, repeating the stand command and preventing the dog from sitting. Once the dog has mastered the stand, teach him to stay by holding him in position and repeating the word "Stay!"

The "down stay" will prove beneficial in many situations, but especially if you wish to take your dog in the car without confining him to a crate. To teach the "down," have the dog sitting at your side with collar and leash on. If he is a large dog, step forward with the leash in your hand and turn so you face him. Let the leash touch the floor, then step over it with your right foot so it is under the instep of your shoe. Grasping the leash low down with both hands, slowly pull up, saying, "Down!" Hold the leash taut until the dog goes down. Once he responds well, teach the dog to stay in the down position (the down-stay), using the same method as for the sit- and stand-stays.

To teach small dogs the "down," another method may be used. Have the dog sit at your side, then kneel beside him. Reach across his back with your left arm, and take hold of his left front leg close to the body. At the same time, with your right hand take hold of his right front leg close to his body. As you command "Down!" gently lift the legs and place the dog in the down position. Release your hold on his legs and slide your left hand onto his back, repeating, "Down, stay," while keeping him in position.

The "come" is taught when the dog is on leash and heeling. Simply walk along, then suddenly take a step backward, saying "Come!" Pull the leash as you give the command and the dog will turn and follow you. Continue walking backward, repeatedly saying "Come," and tightening the leash if necessary.

Once the dog has mastered the exercises while on leash, try taking the leash off and going through the same routine, beginning with the heeling exercise. If the dog doesn't respond promptly, he needs review with the leash on. But patience and persistence will be rewarded, for you will have a dog you can trust to respond promptly under all conditions.

Even after they are well trained, dogs sometimes develop bad habits that are hard to break. Jumping on people is a common habit, and all members of the family must assist if it is to be broken. If the dog is a large or medium breed, take a step for-

ward and raise your knee just as he starts to jump on you. As your knee strikes the dog's chest, command "Down!" in a scolding voice. When a small dog jumps on you, take both front paws in your hands, and, while talking in a pleasant tone of voice, step on the dog's back feet just hard enough to hurt them slightly. With either method the dog is taken by surprise and doesn't associate the discomfort with the person causing it.

Occasionally a dog may be too chummy with guests who don't care for dogs. If the dog has had obedience training, simply command "Come!" When he responds, have him sit beside you.

Excessive barking is likely to bring complaints from neighbors, and persistent efforts may be needed to subdue a dog that barks without provocation. To correct the habit, you must be close to the dog when he starts barking. Encircle his muzzle with both hands, hold his mouth shut, and command "Quiet!" in a firm voice. He should soon learn to respond so you can control him simply by giving the command.

Sniffing other dogs is an annoying habit. If the dog is off leash and sniffs other dogs, ignoring your commands to come, he needs to review the lessons on basic behavior. When the dog is on leash, scold him, then pull on the leash, command "Heel," and walk away from the other dog.

A well-trained dog will be no problem if you decide to take him with you when you travel. No matter how well he responds, however, he should never be permitted off leash when you walk him in a strange area. Distractions will be more tempting, and there will be more chance of his being attacked by other dogs. So whenever the dog travels with you, take his collar and leash along—and use them.

Bench Shows

Centuries ago, it was common practice to hold agricultural fairs in conjunction with spring and fall religious festivals, and to these gatherings, cattle, dogs, and other livestock were brought for exchange. As time went on, it became customary to provide entertainment, too. Dogs often participated in such sporting events as bull baiting, bear baiting, and ratting. Then the dog that exhibited the greatest skill in the arena was also the one that brought the highest price when time came for barter or sale. Today, these fairs seem a far cry from our highly organized bench shows and field trials. But they were the forerunners of modern dog shows and played an important role in shaping the development of purebred dogs.

The first organized dog show was held at Newcastle, England, in 1859. Later that same year, a show was held at Birmingham. At both shows dogs were divided into four classes and only Pointers and Setters were entered. In 1860, the first dog show in Germany was held at Apoldo, where nearly one hundred dogs were exhibited and entries were divided into six groups. Interest expanded rapidly, and by the time the Paris Exhibition was held in 1878, the dog show was a fixture of international importance.

In the United States, the first organized bench show was held in 1874 in conjunction with the meeting of the Illinois State Sportsmen's Association in Chicago, and all entries were dogs of sporting breeds. Although the show was a rather casual affair, interest spread quickly. Before the end of the year, shows were held in Oswego, New York, Mineola, Long Island, and Memphis, Tennessee. And the latter combined a bench show with the first organized field trial ever held in the United States. In January 1875, an all-breed show (the first in the United States) was held at Detroit, Michigan. From then on, interest increased rapidly, though rules were not always uniform, for there was no organization through which to coordinate activities until September 1884

Benching area at Westminster Kennel Club Show.

Judging for Best in Show at Westminster Kennel Club Show.

when The American Kennel Club was founded. Now the largest dog registering organization in the world, the A.K.C. is an association of several hundred member clubs—all breed, specialty, field trial, and obedience groups—each represented by a delegate to the A.K.C.

The several thousand shows and trials held annually in the United States do much to stimulate interest in breeding to produce better looking, sounder, purebred dogs. For breeders, shows provide a means of measuring the merits of their work as compared with accomplishments of other breeders. For hundreds of thousands of dog fanciers, they provide an absorbing hobby.

For both spectators and participating owners, field trials constitute a fascinating demonstration of dogs competing under actual hunting conditions, where emphasis is on excellence of performance. The trials are sponsored by clubs or associations of persons interested in hunting dogs. Trials for Pointing breeds, Dachshunds, Retrievers, Spaniels, and Beagles are under the jurisdiction of The American Kennel Club and information concerning such activities is published in "Pure Bred Dogs—American Kennel Gazette." Trials for Bird Dogs are run by rules and regulations of the Amateur Field Trial Clubs of America and information concerning them is published in "The American Field."

All purebred dogs of recognized breeds may be registered with The American Kennel Club and those of hunting breeds may also be registered with The American Field. Dogs that have won championships both in the field and in bench shows are known as dual champions.

At bench (or conformation) shows, dogs are rated comparatively on their physical qualities (or conformation) in accordance with breed Standards which have been approved by The American Kennel Club. Characteristics such as size, coat, color, placement of eye or ear, general soundness, etc., are the basis for selecting the best dog in a class. Only purebred dogs are eligible to compete and if the show is one where points toward a championship are to be awarded, a dog must be at least six months old.

Bench shows are of various types. An all-breed show has classes for all of the breeds recognized by The American Kennel Club as well as a Miscellaneous Class for breeds not recognized, such as the Australian Cattle Dog, the Ibizan Hound, the Spinoni Italiani, the Tibetan Terrier, etc. A sanctioned match is an informal meeting

where dogs compete but not for championship points. A specialty show is confined to a single breed. Other shows may restrict entries to champions of record, to American-bred dogs, etc. Competition for Junior Showmanship or for Best Brace, Best Team, or Best Local Dog may be included. Also, obedience competition is held in conjunction with many bench shows.

The term "bench show" is somewhat confusing in that shows of this type may be either "benched" or "unbenched." At the former, each dog is assigned an individual numbered stall where he must remain throughout the show except for times when he is being judged, groomed, or exercised. At unbenched shows, no stalls are provided and dogs are kept in their owners' cars or in crates when not being judged.

A show where a dog is judged for conformation actually constitutes an elimination contest. To begin with, the dogs of a single breed compete with others of their breed in one of the regular classes: Puppy, Novice, Bred by Exhibitor, American-Bred, or Open, and, finally, Winners, where the top dogs of the preceding five classes meet. The next step is the judging for Best of Breed (or Best of Variety of Breed). Here the Winners Dog and Winners Bitch (or the dog named Winners if only one prize is awarded) compete with any champions that are entered, together with any undefeated dogs that have competed in additional non-regular classes. The dog named Best of Breed (or Best of Variety of Breed), then goes on to compete with the other Best of Breed winners in his Group. The dogs that win in Group competition then compete for the final and highest honor, Best in Show.

When the Winners Class is divided by sex, championship points are awarded the Winners Dog and Winners Bitch. If the Winners Class is not divided by sex, championship points are awarded the dog or bitch named Winners. The number of points awarded varies, depending upon such factors as the number of dogs competing, the Schedule of Points established by the Board of Directors of the A.K.C., and whether the dog goes on to win Best of Breed, the Group, and Best in Show.

In order to become a champion, a dog must win fifteen points, including points from at least two major wins—that is, at least two shows where three or more points are awarded. The major wins must be under two different judges, and one or more of the remaining points must be won under a third judge. The most points ever awarded at a show is five and the least is one, so, in order to become

Junior Showmanship Competition at Westminster Kennel Club Show.

a champion, a dog must be exhibited and win in at least three shows, and usually he is shown many times before he wins his championship.

"Pure Bred Dogs—American Kennel Gazette" and other dog magazines contain lists of forthcoming shows, together with names and addresses of sponsoring organizations to which you may write for entry forms and information relative to fees, closing dates, etc. Before entering your dog in a show for the first time, you should familiarize yourself with the regulations and rules governing competition. You may secure such information from The American Kennel Club or from a local dog club specializing in your breed. It is essential that you also familiarize yourself with the A.K.C. approved Standard for your breed so you will be fully aware of characteristics worthy of merit as well as those considered faulty, or possibly even serious enough to disqualify the dog from competition. For instance, monorchidism (failure of one testicle to descend) and cryptorchidism (failure of both testicles to descend) are disqualifying faults in all breeds.

If possible, you should first attend a show as a spectator and observe judging procedures from ringside. It will also be helpful to join a local breed club and to participate in sanctioned matches before entering an all-breed show.

The dog should be equipped with a narrow leather show lead and a show collar—never an ornamented or spiked collar. For benched

shows, a metal-link bench chain will be needed to fasten the dog to the bench. For unbenched shows, the dog's crate should be taken along so that he may be confined in comfort when he is not appearing in the ring. A dog should never be left in a car with all the windows closed. In hot weather the temperature will become unbearable in a very short time. Heat exhaustion may result from even a short period of confinement, and death may ensue.

Food and water dishes will be needed, as well as a supply of the food and water to which the dog is accustomed. Brushes and combs are also necessary, so that you may give the dog's coat a final grooming after you arrive at the show.

Familiarize yourself with the schedule of classes ahead of time, for the dog must be fed and exercised and permitted to relieve himself, and any last-minute grooming completed before his class is called. Both you and the dog should be ready to enter the ring unhurriedly. A good deal of skill in conditioning, training, and handling is required if a dog is to be presented properly. And it is essential that the handler himself be composed, for a jittery handler will transmit his nervousness to his dog.

Once the class is assembled in the ring, the judge will ask that the dogs be paraded in line, moving counter-clockwise in a circle. If you have trained your dog well, you will have no difficulty controlling him in the ring, where he must change pace quickly and gracefully and walk and trot elegantly and proudly with head erect. The show dog must also stand quietly for inspection, posing like a statue for several minutes while the judge observes his structure in detail, examines teeth, feet, coat, etc. When the judge calls your dog forward for individual inspection, do not attempt to converse, but answer any questions he may ask.

As the judge examines the class, he measures each dog against the ideal described in the Standard, then measures the dogs against each other in a comparative sense and selects for first place the dog that comes closest to conforming to the Standard for its breed. If your dog isn't among the winners, don't grumble. If he places first, don't brag loudly. For a bad loser is disgusting, but a poor winner is insufferable.

Obedience Competition

For hundreds of years, dogs have been used in England and Germany in connection with police and guard work, and their working potential has been evaluated through tests devised to show agility, strength, and courage. Organized training has also been popular with English and German breeders for many years, although it was first practiced primarily for the purpose of training large breeds in aggressive tactics.

There was little interest in obedience training in the United States until 1933 when Mrs. Whitehouse Walker returned from England and enthusiastically introduced the sport. Two years later, Mrs. Walker persuaded The American Kennel Club to approve organized obedience activities and to assume jurisdiction over obedience rules. Since then, interest has increased at a phenomenal rate, for obedience competition is not only a sport the average spectator can follow readily, but also a sport for which the average owner can train his own dog easily. Obedience competition is suitable for all breeds. Furthermore, there is no limit to the number of dogs that may win in competition, for each dog is scored individually on the basis of a point rating system.

The dog is judged on his response to certain commands, and if he gains a high enough score in three successive trials under different judges, he wins an obedience degree. Degrees awarded are "C.D."—Companion Dog; "C.D.X."—Companion Dog Excellent; and "U.D."—Utility Dog. A fourth degree, the "T.D.," or Tracking Dog degree, may be won at any time and tests for it are held apart from dog shows. The qualifying score is a minimum of 170 points out of a possible total of 200, with no score in any one exercise less than 50% of the points allotted.

Since obedience titles are progressive, earlier titles (with the exception of the tracking degree) are dropped as a dog acquires the next higher degree. If an obedience title is gained in another country in addition to the United States, that fact is signified by the word "International," followed by the title.

Trials for obedience trained dogs are held at most of the larger bench shows, and obedience training clubs are to be found in almost

all communities today. Information concerning forthcoming trials and lists of obedience training clubs are included regularly in "Pure Bred Dogs—American Kennel Gazette"—and other dog magazines. Pamphlets containing rules and regulations governing obedience competition are available upon request from The American Kennel Club, 51 Madison Avenue, New York, N.Y. 10010. Rules are revised occasionally, so if you are interested in participating in obedience competition, you should be sure your copy of the regulations is current.

All dogs must comply with the same rules, although in broad jump, high jump, and bar jump competition, the jumps are adjusted to the size of the breed. Classes at obedience trials are divided into Novice (A and B), Open (A and B), and Utility (which may be divided into A and B, at the option of the sponsoring club and with the approval of The American Kennel Club).

The Novice class is for dogs that have not won the title Companion Dog. In Novice A, no person who has previously handled a dog that has won a C.D. title in the obedience ring at a licensed or member trial, and no person who has regularly trained such a dog, may enter or handle a dog. The handler must be the dog's owner or a member of the owner's immediate family. In Novice B, dogs may be handled by the owner or any other person.

The Open A class is for dogs that have won the C.D. title but have not won the C.D.X. title. Obedience judges and licensed handlers may not enter or handle dogs in this class. Each dog must be handled by the owner or by a member of his immediate family. The Open B class is for dogs that have won the title C.D. or C.D.X. A dog may continue to compete in this class after it has won the title U.D. Dogs in this class may be handled by the owner or any other person.

The Utility class is for dogs that have won the title C.D.X. Dogs that have won the title U.D. may continue to compete in this class, and dogs may be handled by the owner or any other person. Provided the A.K.C. approves, a club may choose to divide the Utility class into Utility A and Utility B. When this is done, the Utility A class is for dogs that have won the title C.D.X. and have not won the title U.D. Obedience judges and licensed handlers may not enter or handle dogs in this class. All other dogs that are eligible for the Utility class but not eligible for Utility A may be entered in Utility B.

Novice competition includes such exercises as heeling on and off lead, the stand for examination, coming on recall, and the long sit and the long down.

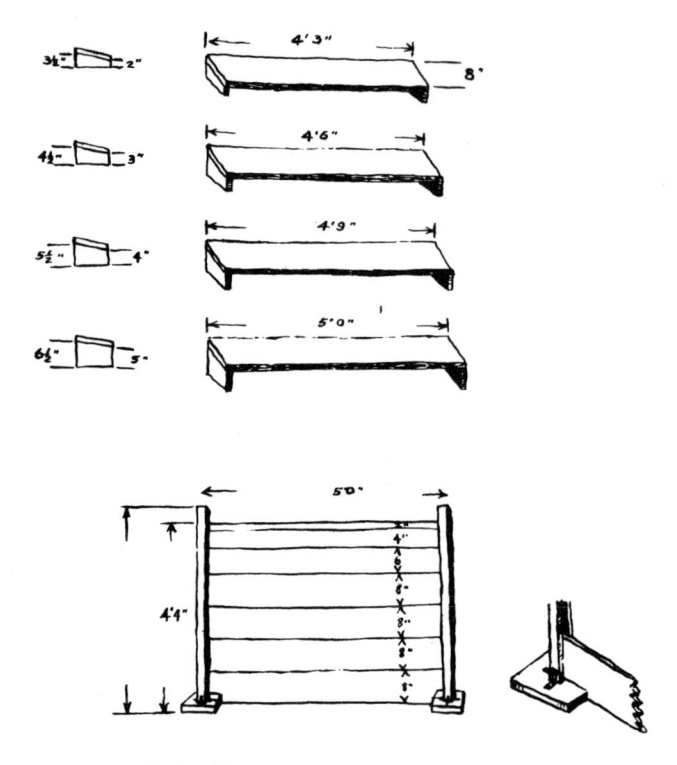

Broad jump and solid hurdle.

In Open competition, the dog must perform such exercises as heeling free, the drop on recall, and the retrieve on the flat and over the high jump. Also, he must execute the broad jump, and the long sit and long down.

In the Utility class, competition includes scent discrimination, the directed retrieve, the signal exercise, directed jumping, and the group examination.

Tracking is the most difficult test. It is always done out-of-doors, of course, and, for obvious reasons, cannot be held at a dog show. The dog must follow a scent trail that is about a quarter mile in length. He is also required to find a scent object (glove, wallet, or other article) left by a stranger who has walked the course to lay down the scent. The dog is required to follow the trail a half to two hours after the scent is laid.

An ideal way to train a dog for obedience competition is to join an obedience class or a training club. In organized class work, beginners' classes cover pretty much the same exercises as those

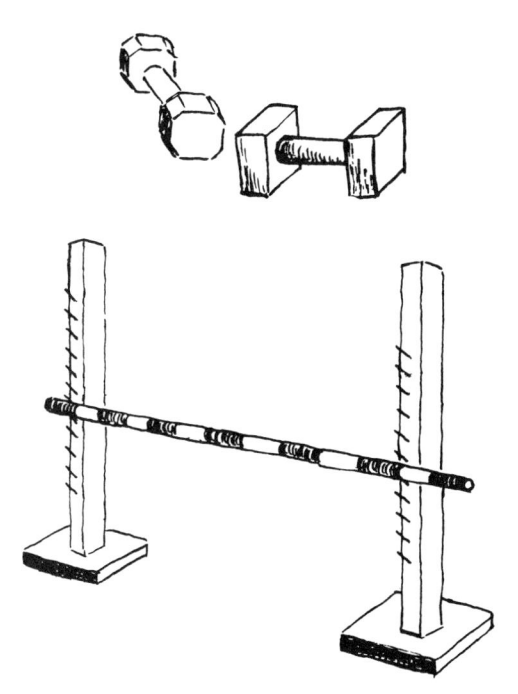

Dumbbells and bar jump.

described in the chapter on training. However, through class work you will develop greater precision than is possible in training your dog by yourself. Amateur handlers often cause the dog to be penalized, for if the handler fails to abide by the rules, it is the dog that suffers the penalty. A common infraction of the rules is using more than one signal or command where regulations stipulate only one may be used. Classwork will help eliminate such errors, which the owner may make unconsciously if he is working alone. Working with a class will also acquaint both dog and handler with ring procedure so that obedience trials will not present unforeseen problems.

Thirty or forty owners and dogs often comprise a class, and exercises are performed in unison, with individual instruction provided if it is required. The procedure followed in training—in fact, even wording of various commands—may vary from instructor to instructor. Equipment used will vary somewhat, also, but will usually include a training collar and leash such as those shown on page 109, a long line, a dumbbell, and a jumping stick.

The latter may be a short length of heavy doweling or a broom handle and both it and the dumbbell are usually painted white for increased visibility.

A bitch in season must never be taken to a training class, so before enrolling a female dog, you should determine whether she may be expected to come into season before classes are scheduled to end. If you think she will, it is better to wait and enroll her in a later course, rather than start the course and then miss classes for several weeks.

In addition to the time devoted to actual work in class, the dog must have regular, daily training sessions for practice at home. Before each class or home training session, the dog should be exercised so he will not be highly excited when the session starts, and he must be given an opportunity to relieve himself before the session begins. (Should he have an accident during the class, it is your responsibility to clean up after him.) The dog should be fed several hours before time for the class to begin or else after the class is over—never just before going to class.

If you decide to enter your dog in obedience competition, it is well to enter a small, informal show the first time. Dogs are usually called in the order in which their names appear in the catalog, so as soon as you arrive at the show, acquaint yourself with the schedule. If your dog is not the first to be judged, spend some time at ringside, observing the routine so you will know what to expect when your dog's turn comes.

In addition to collar, leash, and other equipment, you should take your dog's food and water pans and a supply of the food and water to which he is accustomed. You should also take his brushes and combs in order to give him a last-minute brushing before you enter the ring. It is important that the dog look his best even though he isn't to be judged on his appearance.

Before entering the ring, exercise your dog, give him a drink of water, and permit him to relieve himself. Once your dog enters the ring, give him your full attention and be sure to give voice commands distinctly so he will hear and understand, for there will be many distractions at ringside.

Top dogs in Utility Class. This illustrates variety of breeds that compete in obedience.

Genetics

Genetics, the science of heredity, deals with the processes by which physical and mental traits of parents are transmitted to offspring. For centuries, man has been trying to solve these puzzles, but only in the last two hundred years has significant progress been made.

During the eighteenth century, Kölreuter, a German scientist, made revolutionary discoveries concerning plant sexuality and hybridization but was unable to explain just how hereditary processes worked. In the middle of the nineteenth century, Gregor Johann Mendel, an Augustinian monk, experimented with the ordinary garden pea and made other discoveries of major significance. He found that an inherited characteristic was inherited as a complete unit, and that certain characteristics predominated over others. Next, he observed that the hereditary characteristics of each parent are contained in each offspring, even when they are not visible, and that "hidden" characteristics can be transferred without change in their nature to the grandchildren, or even later generations. Finally, he concluded that although heredity contains an element of uncertainty, some things are predictable on the basis of well-defined mathematical laws.

Unfortunately, Mendel's published paper went unheeded, and when he died in 1884 he was still virtually unknown to the scientific world. But other researchers were making discoveries, too. In 1900, three different scientists reported to learned societies that much of their research in hereditary principles had been proved years before by Gregor Mendel and that findings matched perfectly.

Thus, hereditary traits were proved to be transmitted through the chromosomes found in pairs in every living being, one of each pair contributed by the mother, the other by the father. Within each chromosome have been found hundreds of smaller structures, or genes, which are the actual determinants of hereditary characteristics. Some genes are dominant and will be seen

in the offspring. Others are recessive and will not be outwardly apparent, yet can be passed on to the offspring to combine with a similar recessive gene of the other parent and thus be seen. Or they may be passed on to the offspring, not be outwardly apparent, but be passed on again to become apparent in a later generation.

Once the genetic theory of inheritance became widely known, scientists began drawing a well-defined line between inheritance and environment. More recent studies show some overlapping of these influences and indicate a combination of the two may be responsible for certain characteristics. For instance, studies have proved that extreme cold increases the amount of black pigment in the skin and hair of the "Himalayan" rabbit, although it has little or no effect on the white or colored rabbit. Current research also indicates that even though characteristics are determined by the genes, some environmental stress occurring at a particular period of pregnancy might cause physical change in the embryo.

Long before breeders had any knowledge of genetics, they practiced one of its most important principles—selective breeding. Experience quickly showed that "like begets like," and by breeding like with like and discarding unlike offspring, the various individual breeds were developed to the point where variations were relatively few. Selective breeding is based on the idea of maintaining the quality of a breed at the highest possible level, while improving whatever defects are prevalent. It requires that only the top dogs in a litter be kept for later breeding, and that inferior specimens be ruthlessly eliminated.

In planning any breeding program, the first requisite is a definite goal—that is, to have clearly in mind a definite picture of the type of dog you wish eventually to produce. To attempt to breed perfection is to approach the problem unrealistically. But if you don't breed for improvement, it is preferable that you not breed at all.

As a first step, you should select a bitch that exemplifies as many of the desired characteristics as possible and mate her with a dog that also has as many of the desired characteristics as possible. If you start with mediocre pets, you will produce mediocre pet puppies. If you decide to start with more than one bitch, all should closely approach the type you desire, since you will

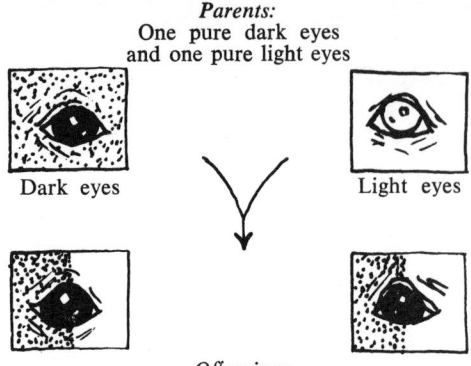

Parents:
One pure dark eyes
and one pure light eyes

Dark eyes — Light eyes

Offspring:
Eyes dark (dominant) with light recessive

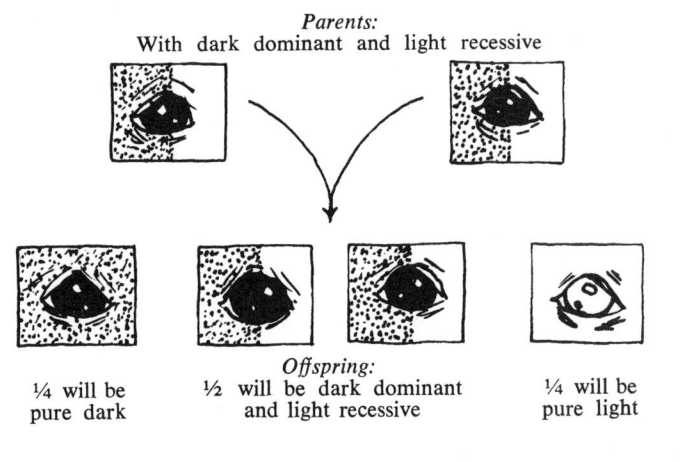

Parents:
With dark dominant and light recessive

¼ will be pure dark — ½ will be dark dominant and light recessive — ¼ will be pure light

Offspring:

The above is a schematic representation of the Mendelian law as it applies to the inheritance of eye color. The law applies in the same way to the inheritance of other physical characteristics.

then stand a better chance of producing uniformly good puppies from all. Breeders often start with a single bitch and keep the best bitches in every succeeding generation.

Experienced breeders look for "prepotency" in breeding stock —that is, the ability of a dog or bitch to transmit traits to most or all of its offspring. While the term is usually used to describe the transmission of good qualities, a dog may also be prepotent in transmitting faults. To be prepotent in a practical sense, a dog must possess many characteristics controlled by dominant genes. If desired characteristics are recessive, they will be apparent in

the offspring only if carried by both sire and dam. Prepotent dogs and bitches usually come from a line of prepotent ancestors, but the mere fact that a dog has exceptional ancestors will not necessarily mean that he himself will produce exceptional offspring.

A single dog may sire a tremendous number of puppies, whereas a bitch can produce only a comparatively few litters during her lifetime. Thus, a sire's influence may be very widespread as compared to that of a bitch. But in evaluating a particular litter, it must be remembered that the bitch has had as much influence as has had the dog.

Inbreeding, line-breeding, outcrossing, or a combination of the three are the methods commonly used in selective breeding.

Inbreeding is the mating together of closely related animals, such as father-daughter, mother-son, or brother-sister. Although some breeders insist such breeding will lead to the production of defective individuals, it is through rigid inbreeding that all breeds of dogs have been established. Controlled tests have shown that any harmful effects appear within the first five or ten generations, and that if rigid selection is exercised from the beginning, a vigorous inbred strain will be built up.

Line-breeding is also the mating together of individuals related by family lines. However, matings are made not so much on the basis of the dog's and bitch's relationship to each other, but, instead, on the basis of their relationship to a highly admired ancestor, with a view to perpetuating his qualities. Line-breeding constitutes a long-range program and cannot be accomplished in a single generation.

Outcrossing is the breeding together of two dogs that are unrelated in family lines. Actually, since breeds have been developed through the mating of close relatives, all dogs within any given breed are related to some extent. There are few breedings that are true outcrosses, but if there is no common ancestor within five generations, a mating is usually considered an outcross.

Experienced breeders sometimes outcross for one generation in order to eliminate a particular fault, then go back to inbreeding or line-breeding. Neither the good effects nor the bad effects of outcrossing can be truly evaluated in a single mating, for undesirable recessive traits may be introduced into a strain, yet

not show up for several generations. Outcrossing is better left to experienced breeders, for continual outcrossing results in a wide variation in type and great uncertainty as to the results that may be expected.

Two serious defects that are believed heritable—subluxation and orchidism—should be zealously guarded against, and afflicted dogs and their offspring should be eliminated from breeding programs. Subluxation is a condition of the hip joint where the bone of the socket is eroded and the head of the thigh bone is also worn away, causing lameness which becomes progressively more serious until the dog is unable to walk. Orchidism is the failure of one or both testicles to develop and descend properly. When one testicle is involved, the term "monorchid" is used. When both are involved, "cryptorchid" is used. A cryptorchid is almost always sterile, whereas a monorchid is usually fertile. There is evidence that orchidism "runs in families" and that a monorchid transmits the tendency through bitch and male puppies alike.

Through the years, many misconceptions concerning heredity have been perpetuated. Perhaps the one most widely perpetuated is the idea evolved hundreds of years ago that somehow characteristics were passed on through the mixing of the blood of the parents. We still use terminology evolved from that theory when we speak of bloodlines, or describe individuals as full-blooded, despite the fact that the theory was disproved more than a century ago.

Also inaccurate and misleading is any statement that a definite fraction or proportion of an animal's inherited characteristics can be positively attributed to a particular ancestor. Individuals lacking knowledge of genetics sometimes declare that an individual receives half his inherited characteristics from each parent, a quarter from each grandparent, an eighth from each great-grandparent, etc. Thousands of volumes of scientific findings have been published, but no simple way has been found to determine positively which characteristics have been inherited from which ancestors, for the science of heredity is infinitely complex.

Any breeder interested in starting a serious breeding program should study several of the excellent books on canine genetics that are currently available.

Whelping box. Detail at right shows proper side-wall construction which helps keep small puppies confined and provides sheltered nook which to prevent crushing or smothering.

Breeding and Whelping

The breeding life of a bitch begins when she comes into season the first time at the age of about one to two years (depending on what breed she is). Thereafter, she will come in season at roughly six-month intervals, but this, too, is subject to variation. Her maximum fertility builds up from puberty to full maturity and then declines until a state of total sterility is reached in old age. Just when this occurs is hard to determine, for the fact that an older bitch shows signs of being in season doesn't necessarily mean she is still capable of reproducing.

The length of the season varies from eighteen to twenty-one days. The first indication is a pronounced swelling of the vulva with coincidental bleeding (called "showing color") for about the first seven to nine days. The discharge gradually turns to a creamy color, and it is during this phase (estrus), from about the tenth to the fifteenth days, that the bitch is ovulating and is receptive to the male. The ripe, unfertilized ova survive for about seventy-two hours. If fertilization doesn't occur, the ova die and are discharged the next time the bitch comes in season. If fertilization does take place, each ovum attaches itself to the walls of the uterus, a membrane forms to seal it off, and a foetus develops from it.

Following the estrus phase, the bitch is still in season until about the twenty-first day and will continue to be attractive to males, although she will usually fight them off as she did the first few days. Nevertheless, to avoid accidental mating, the bitch must be confined for the entire period. Virtual imprisonment is necessary, for male dogs display uncanny abilities in their efforts to reach a bitch in season.

The odor that attracts the males is present in the bitch's urine, so it is advisable to take her a good distance from the house before permitting her to relieve herself. To eliminate problems completely, your veterinarian can prescribe a preparation that will disguise the odor but will not interfere with breeding when the time is right. Many fanciers use such preparations when exhibit-

ing a bitch and find that nearby males show no interest whatsoever. But it is not advisable to permit a bitch to run loose when she has been given a product of this type, for during estrus she will seek the company of male dogs and an accidental mating may occur.

A potential brood bitch, regardless of breed, should have good bone, ample breadth and depth of ribbing, and adequate room in the pelvic region. Unless a bitch is physically mature—well beyond the puppy stage when she has her first season—breeding should be delayed until her second or a later season. Furthermore, even though it is possible for a bitch to conceive twice a year, she should not be bred oftener than once a year. A bitch that is bred too often will age prematurely and her puppies are likely to lack vigor.

Two or three months before a bitch is to be mated, her physical condition should be considered carefully. If she is too thin, provide a rich, balanced diet plus the regular exercise needed to develop strong, supple muscles. Daily exercise on the lead is as necessary for the too-thin bitch as for the too fat one, although the latter will need more exercise and at a brisker pace, as well as a reduction of food, if she is to be brought to optimum condition. A prospective brood bitch must have had permanent distemper shots as well as rabies vaccination. And a month before her season is due, a veterinarian should examine a stool specimen for worms. If there is evidence of infestation, the bitch should be wormed.

A dog may be used at stud from the time he reaches physical maturity, well on into old age. The first time your bitch is bred, it is well to use a stud that has already proven his ability by having sired other litters. The fact that a neighbor's dog is readily available should not influence your choice, for to produce the best puppies, you must select the stud most suitable from a genetic standpoint.

If the stud you prefer is not going to be available at the time your bitch is to be in season, you may wish to consult your veterinarian concerning medications available for inhibiting the onset of the season. With such preparations, the bitch's season can be delayed indefinitely.

Usually the first service will be successful. However, if it isn't,

in most cases an additional service is given free, provided the stud dog is still in the possession of the same owner. If the bitch misses, it may be because her cycle varies widely from normal. Through microscopic examination, a veterinarian can determine exactly when the bitch is entering the estrus phase and thus is likely to conceive.

The owner of the stud should give you a stud-service certificate, providing a four-generation pedigree for the sire and showing the date of mating. The litter registration application is completed only after the puppies are whelped, but it, too, must be signed by the owner of the stud as well as the owner of the bitch. Registration forms may be secured by writing The American Kennel Club.

In normal pregnancy there is usually visible enlargement of the abdomen by the end of the fifth week. By palpation (feeling with the fingers) a veterinarian may be able to distinguish developing puppies as early as three weeks after mating, but it is unwise for a novice to poke and prod, and try to detect the presence of unborn puppies.

The gestation period normally lasts nine weeks, although it may vary from sixty-one to sixty-five days. If it goes beyond sixty-five days from the date of mating, a veterinarian should be consulted.

During the first four or five weeks, the bitch should be permitted her normal amount of activity. As she becomes heavier, she should be walked on the lead, but strenuous running and jumping should be avoided. Her diet should be well balanced (see page 43), and if she should become constipated, small amounts of mineral oil may be added to her food.

A whelping box should be secured about two weeks before the puppies are due, and the bitch should start then to use it as her bed so she will be accustomed to it by the time puppies arrive. Preferably, the box should be square, with each side long enough so that the bitch can stretch out full length and have several inches to spare at either end. The bottom should be padded with an old cotton rug or other material that is easily laundered. Edges of the padding should be tacked to the floor of the box so the puppies will not get caught in it and smother. Once it is obvious labor is about to begin, the padding should be covered with

several layers of spread-out newspapers. Then, as papers become soiled, the top layer can be pulled off, leaving the area clean.

Forty-eight to seventy-two hours before the litter is to be whelped, a definite change in the shape of the abdomen will be noted. Instead of looking barrel-shaped, the abdomen will sag pendulously. Breasts usually redden and become enlarged, and milk may be present a day or two before the puppies are whelped. As the time becomes imminent, the bitch will probably scratch and root at her bedding in an effort to make a nest, and will refuse food and ask to be let out every few minutes. But the surest sign is a drop in temperature of two or three degrees about twelve hours before labor begins.

The bitch's abdomen and flanks will contract sharply when labor actually starts, and for a few minutes she will attempt to expel a puppy, then rest for a while and try again. Someone should stay with the bitch the entire time whelping is taking place, and if she appears to be having unusual difficulties, a veterinarian should be called.

Puppies are usually born head first, though some may be born feet first and no difficulty encountered. Each puppy is enclosed in a separate membranous sac that the bitch will remove with her teeth. She will sever the umbilical cord, which will be attached to the soft, spongy afterbirth that is expelled right after the puppy emerges. Usually the bitch eats the afterbirth, so it is necessary to watch and make sure one is expelled for each puppy whelped. If afterbirth is retained, the bitch may develop peritonitis and die.

The dam will lick and nuzzle each newborn puppy until it is warm and dry and ready to nurse. If puppies arrive so close together that she can't take care of them, you can help her by rubbing the puppies dry with a soft .cloth. If several have been whelped but the bitch continues to be in labor, all but one should be removed and placed in a small box lined with clean towels and warmed to about seventy degrees. The bitch will be calmer if one puppy is left with her at all times.

Whelping sometimes continues as long as twenty-four hours for a very large litter, but a litter of two or three puppies may be whelped in an hour. When the bitch settles down, curls around the puppies and nuzzles them to her, it usually indicates that all have been whelped.

The bitch should be taken away for a few minutes while you clean the box and arrange clean padding. If her coat is soiled, sponge it clean before she returns to the puppies. Once she is back in the box, offer her a bowl of warm beef broth and a pan of cool water, placing both where she will not have to get up in order to reach them. As soon as she indicates interest in food, give her a generous bowl of chopped meat to which codliver oil and dicalcium phosphate have been added (see page 43).

If inadequate amounts of calcium are provided during the period the puppies are nursing, eclampsia may develop. Symptoms are violent trembling, rapid rise in temperature, and rigidity of muscles. Veterinary assistance must be secured immediately, for death may result in a very short time. Treatment consists of massive doses of calcium gluconate administered intravenously, after which symptoms subside in a miraculously short time.

All puppies are born blind and their eyes open when they are ten to fourteen days old. At first the eyes have a bluish cast and appear weak, and the puppies must be protected from strong light until at least ten days after the eyes open.

To ensure proper emotional development, young dogs should be shielded from loud noises and rough handling. Being lifted by the front legs is painful and may result in permanent injury to the shoulders. So when lifting a puppy, always place one hand under the chest with the forefinger between the front legs, and place the other hand under his bottom.

Sometimes the puppies' nails are so long and sharp that they scratch the bitch's breasts. Since the nails are soft, they can be trimmed with ordinary scissors.

If of a breed that ordinarily has a docked tail, puppies should have their tails shortened when they are three days old. Dewclaws—thumblike appendages appearing on the inside of the legs of some breeds—are removed at the same time. While both are simple procedures, they shouldn't be attempted by amateurs.

In certain breeds it is customary to crop the ears, also. This should be done at about eight weeks of age. Cropping should never be attempted by anyone other than a veterinarian, for it requires use of anesthesia and knowledge of surgical techniques, as well as judgment as to the eventual size of the dog and pro-

portion of ear to be removed so the head will be balanced when the dog is mature.

At about four weeks of age, formula should be provided. The amount fed each day should be increased over a period of two weeks, when the puppies can be weaned completely. The formula should be prepared as described on page 41, warmed to lukewarm, and poured into a shallow pan placed on the floor of the box. After his mouth has been dipped into the mixture a few times, a puppy will usually start to lap formula. All puppies should be allowed to eat from the same pan, but be sure the small ones get their share. If they are pushed aside, feed them separately. Permit the puppies to nurse part of the time, but gradually increase the number of meals of formula. By the time the puppies are five weeks old, the dam should be allowed with them only at night. When they are about six weeks old, they should be weaned completely and fed the puppy diet described on page 41.

Once they are weaned, puppies should be given temporary distemper injections every two weeks until they are old enough for permanent inoculations. At six weeks, stool specimens should be checked for worms, for almost without exception, puppies become infested. Specimens should be checked again at eight weeks, and as often thereafter as your veterinarian recommends.

Sometimes owners decide as a matter of convenience to have a bitch spayed or a male castrated. While this is recommended when a dog has a serious inheritable defect or when abnormalities of reproductive organs develop, in sound, normal purebred dogs, spaying a bitch or castrating a male may prove a definite disadvantage. The operations automatically bar dogs from competing in shows as well as precluding use for breeding. The operations are seldom dangerous, but they should not be performed without good reason.

Personality of the Springer

Once the personality of the Springer Spaniel touches a person, it leaves a mark that seldom wears off. Undoubtedly you know people who have been involved with dogs of various breeds, going from one breed to another—perhaps just to own winners. But if you sit down to talk with these people about dogs, they usually become most lyrical concerning the Springer they owned at one time and admit it was one of the finest dogs they ever had.

A Springer has a way of working into a home and making a niche that will always belong only to a Springer. Once this happens, it never changes. And it is most enjoyable to listen to Springer owners tell you about the one that took over their home—for you know just how they feel.

A Springer has a distinct capability of worming its way into the family, and even owners who never took dogs of other breeds away from home, will start planning vacations they think their Springer will like. And by the time the dog and all his gear are loaded into the station wagon, the owner will definitely know his Springer is going along!

Springers are quick to learn and can be taught many things. With patient instruction, one lesson often is sufficient. When instructing the Springer, it is preferable to make a game of the lesson and to use a single command for each act the Springer is being taught to perform. Take care not to overwork the dog so that the learning ceases to be fun. And be sure to praise him and pet him when he performs well. Springers love hands and the more hands of different people that are laid on them, the better they like it.

I was told years ago that if Springers are reprimanded and talked to about a misdeed, they will seldom make the same mistake again. Experience has proven this to be correct.

In the show ring the Springer should exhibit poise, attentiveness, and tractability, and should allow the judge to examine him without cringing or showing resentment. To develop these qualities, the dog needs some training and encouragement. But anyone who has seen a great champion jump with joy that matches his handler's when the judge points him out as the top winner, knows that the ultimate in

Can., Am., Bda. Ch. Oaktrees Lancashire Poacher, by Can. Ch. Oaktree's Drunken Piper ex Can. Ch. Salilyn's Kissin' Cousin. Exclusive Agent-Handler for "Oaktrees," W. J. Trainor.

show-ring excitement is as great for the dog as it is for the handler.

And the good gun dog reacts the same way in the field. His tail goes lickety-split and his ears flop gaily as he streaks around the field. And when he really gets his nostrils full of bird, he lights up all over and is a joy to watch. Many a gun enthusiast is as content just to work a good dog in the field and watch him get "birdy" as he is to hunt over him.

It doesn't matter which they are, pets, show dogs, or gun dogs, Springers associate so congenially with people that often we wonder if they are humans too. They sense disappointment—they know when they are in the wrong—and they career madly all over the place with joyous abandon when they feel an occasion is a happy one.

Springers soon learn schedules of the home and can almost tell time as they follow these schedules daily. Try packing a car when it's vacation time and if the Springer is to go along, he is the first thing in the car. If he isn't to go along, he can be so downcast that it almost spoils all your fun.

Put a crate in the wagon and try to keep your show Springer from getting out in the wet grass of an early morning and romping madly about while you try to get the rest of the show tack loaded.

Or change into your old gun clothes, take down a gun and drop a few shells into your pocket, and try to keep your gun dog from tearing a hole in the wall or taking a panel out of the kitchen door.

Yes, they are characters, and they have character as well, for they can become sober and quiet should things go wrong in a home. When someone is sick, there will be a head with two very soulful eyes alongside the chair or bed—watching hopefully for some sign of encouragement that matters will soon be fine again. All play is put aside, but—as they assure you—only temporarily, until you are well again. Springers like people and they love to meet and to greet people and to have people fuss over them.

Some years ago, I had a telephone call from a friend whose stud dog had been bred to a bitch and after the whelping the owner of the bitch had kept a dog puppy and a bitch puppy. Under duress, the owner had sold the dog at ten months of age to an executive of a big

Oaktree's Fandangle, Futurity Winner at 1970 EESSC Show, Worcester, Massachusetts. Shown here by Mrs. George Alston for W. J. Trainor.

A well-set-up adult study

industrial plant in Philadelphia. The industrialist took the dog home and a week later asked four friends to go hunting with him and his new "bird" dog. The field was full of birds and the five hunters shot all morning. By noon the pup was cringing, crying, and scared petrified. So he was chucked into the wagon, taken home, and dumped in the yard, where he spent the next two months alone—talked to over the fence only by a neighbor and two children of the owner. Finally, the ultimatum went forth that the food cost was too great for a no-good dog—either find a home for him or have the vet put him down. This by the inexorable master.

His wife called my friend, who called me. As soon as I heard the details of the breeding of the dog, I wanted him, for his sire was a good dog in my estimation and his bloodlines were such that I felt he was well worth salvaging. So we drove to the home of the owner.

We went into the living room and I saw a Springer—his teeth bared —under the dining room table with the two youngsters. My friend and the lady of the house started talking and I sat down. But I asked the older child to let Timmie come over to me if he wanted to. Some time later, Timmie managed to get to me—laid his head on my knee, and we were acquainted. The lady of the house finally looked around, saw us, and screamed, "He'll bite you." But by that time I had hold of his collar and told her I'd take him and give him a good home. She wouldn't believe me when I came back a few minutes later and told her he was in my car. Making sure I had the papers, my friend and I left and I went home.

Since our house is "doggy," Timmie was allowed to ramble over it and we sat down to dinner. He didn't come near us until we were through eating and just sitting and waiting quietly. But he finally came and laid his chin in my lap. Immediately, I got up, spread papers on the living room floor, and took him in and started combing him. When I had finished the combing, I trimmed him. That night he slept next to me on the floor near my bed.

Next morning, after breakfast, we went for a walk. About a half mile from home, at a crossroad, I took him off the lead to see whether or not he was my dog. He romped up the road—happily heading for home.

The oddity of this is that for ten years, "Milbert's Tiny Tim" was top stud at "Recess" and sired some of the finest gun dogs in this end of Pennsylvania. And now, nearly fifteen years later, we still get calls for gun dog puppies related to Timmie. And, as far as I've known, there's not been a gunshy pup in the lot.

World's youngest obedience class (5½ weeks). Litter by Ch. Kaintuck Christmas Carol ex Ch. Cartref Donla's Arpege, C.D., perform "sit-stay" exercise. Laddie, Nicky, Holly, Chris, Lucky, Rudy, Tinsel, and Peter.

The Springer in the Obedience Ring

Obedience competition is one of the most intriguing facets of Springer ownership. From the first, obedience has been "duck soup" for most Springers, for they learn readily what is expected of them, and, being inclined to be as "hammy" as any breed, they love the acclaim accorded them as competitors—not only by their handler in the ring but also by the judge and the gallery.

The exercises a dog learns in order to earn the obedience degrees are described in the chapter beginning on page 111. These exercises make the dog a responsible animal, ready to perform work of any kind. And once absorbed, the training stays with the dog. I have seen obedience-trained Springers put through the exercises years later, and they were still almost unbelievably adept in their performance.

Obedience competition always draws a large audience, and interest in it is increasing rapidly—especially considering that as an adjunct to the sport of dogs, obedience is the youngest branch of shows.

Most Springer clubs have added obedience to their specialty shows, and the parent club added obedience to its agenda in 1959 and also formulated rules and regulations for recognizing Springers excelling in obedience. Jessie Gebert, George Pugh, and Mary Jo Hosteny comprised the committee appointed for this purpose, and certificates of commendation have been given out each year since 1959 at the dinner following the National Specialty Show. Awards based on high score wins made during the year are given for "Springer of the Year" in both Novice and Open Dog and Bitch categories. 1972 marks the fourteenth year that such awards have been made. Most of the dogs winning plaques from the parent club were also big winners at regular obedience trials—point shows and obedience club trials—where they won many times against all breeds. An outstanding example is Bal Lakes Lady Patricia, Obedience Springer of the Year for 1961, 1962, 1963, and 1964, and also winner in twelve all-breed obedience trials, with a perfect score of 200 in eight of them. This great dog consistently averaged between 199 and 200 and set records which may never be broken. She was owned by Edson Bahr, Edmonds, Washington.

Henry of Navarre, C.D., was the first Springer owned by the Becher Hungerfords and became the "sparkplug" for their interest in the breed.

Ch. Cartref Donla's Arpege headed up the winning Brood Bitch Class entry at the EESSC Specialty Show held June 20, 1964—confronting Judge Andrew Klembara with the only twelve-piece Springer Spaniel entry on record! Pictured above (right to left) are Arpege; Ch. Berlytown Knight's Arpeggio, C.D.X. (Mary V. Costello); and Ch. Beryltown Rockette of Rovenn (Richard L. Inman). Below (right to left), are Ch. Beryltown's Steadfast Knight (E. G. R. Bourguignon); Ch. Beryltown Rocketing Bobbie (Carole A. White); Ch. Beryltown Red-Hot Rocket (Dr. Wm. H. Funderburk); Ch. Flaming Ember of Berclee (Bernice C. Roe); and Ch. Beryltown Rocket Rumpus, Am., Can. C.D. (Irene Donovan). Missing out on the picture taking were three other Arpege champions: Ch. Beryltown Lucky Christmas, Ch. Beryltown Lively Rocket, C.D., and Ch. Beryltown Screaming Rocket, C.D.

Now all thoughts are centered on the get of Inchidony Prince Charming and their records, but I'll wager both Hungerfords think many times of the fun they had with Henry of Navarre, C.D.

Ch. Lassie of Kahagan, owned by R. Thompson, Oakland, California, was the first champion bitch to attain an obedience degree. She acquired her Companion Dog degree in 1939 and her Utility Dog degree in 1945. Sally of Duckenfield, owned by Charles A. Frank, Detroit, Michigan, the first Springer bitch to attain the Utility Dog degree, competed in trials for seven years with many first-place wins and one perfect score of 200. At an advanced age, she scored 199 and was Third in a class of forty-nine.

As was stated in an earlier chapter, all puppies from Waiterock Kennels are given obedience and field training before being sold, but Waiterock Callan of Kildare, handled and trained to the sharpest edge by Owner Mary Jo Hosteny, not only acquired top degrees in the United States but in Canada as well.

Victoria of Heidest, owned by Miss Margery Adams, Waban, Massachusetts, was the first Springer to be awarded the title of Utility Dog Tracker. She acquired the title in 1950.

Among the dogs I have watched at various trials in the East were Flightline Flagship, who got his U.D. degree in 1958, and Ch. Beryltown The Mystic Knight, U.D.T., who acquired his in 1964. Both were owned by Corson Jones. The Knight was a dog from the Beryl900n Kennel, where all puppies go through the obedience workshop and then go on to bench activities.

Also among Springers with obedience degrees are Ch. Carey's Brown Bomber, C.D., and Ch. Carey's Prince Michael, C.D., owned by Andrew and Mary Carey. In addition to providing obedience training, the Careys also show their dogs in the conformation ring and train them for the field and for hunting. At most shows the Careys' dogs compete all over the grounds. Carey's Anglo Saxon Bramble, owned by Mr. and Mrs. S. H. Gardner, is another Springer on the U.D. list.

Another terrific performer who was on the parent club commendation list in 1961, 1962, and 1963, was Amand's Tonga, owned, trained, and shown by Harold Weaver, Reading, Pennsylvania. Tonga acquired her U.D.T. and it was interesting to hear tales of how she was used as an official tracking dog by law officers in Berks County, Pennsylvania, in lieu of the usual tracking dogs such as Bloodhounds.

Yes, Springers have held their own in the past thirty-five years of obedience competition, and there have been many instances where

The Carpenter girls and their dogs, Huvals Christmas Knight and Ch. Holly Hills Winged Elm.

Starfoot Kennel Springers, after a swim on a sunny fall day.

Springers made great performances at trials. Conformation exhibitors as well as the general public watch Springer entries in obedience—just as they do in conformation classes—for they realize that the breed is one to be reckoned with at obedience trials as well as in the show ring.

One nice thing about obedience is the fact that it gives additional members of a family a chance to compete with a dog at a show. Teaching a dog obedience often affords the distaff side of the family an opportunity to enjoy the Springer. And children love obedience, for it not only gives them a chance to start showing the dog but also gives them a great feeling of togetherness when they work in obedience with their dog.

Dogs can be entered at match and point shows so that they have plenty of opportunity to perfect their work and steady down before they start competing for degrees. Such shows give the exhibitor opportunities to check every move made by his dog so that any necessary corrections in technique may be made.

Obedience classes afford newcomers in dogs an opportunity to help their dogs and also provide a good means of meeting other dog owners and seeing other breeds. Thus, owners not only increase their dogs' knowledge but also increase their own knowledge of dogs.

There is not so much stress placed on the lineage of a Springer in obedience, but the training is a definite aid to establishing an added worth to the dog. Many kennels place great importance on obedience for their dogs. These kennels claim that their dogs consistently have great dispositions as a result of their obedience training, and it usually works that very way.

Some kennels use portions of the obedience training routine to train their dogs to do special things that make them stand out, and this also helps the dogs as pets or as show dogs. Many gun dog and field dog enthusiasts also provide obedience training for their Springers, for they find it helpful in working the dog in the field.

Sir Casey of Lyme Rock and Owner-Handler Harold L. Hall at Keystone English Springer Spaniel Club Trial, 1970.

Cliff Wallace during a tense moment at 1970 Keystone Trial.

The Springer in the Field

Discussing field dogs in England as opposed to field dogs in America, one authority says that it is regrettable that the show dog owners in England would not mate their bitches with field dogs, so that the slower show dog could produce pups with something of the keen intelligence, quick movement, and style of the field dog, or, on the other side, so that the small, very often plain headed working dog could acquire a more recognizable Springer appearance.

We in the United States started down that road years back with imports of field dogs from England. At the same time, we had many kennels in America breeding both show and field types. The result was that we had a split, but we are considerably ahead of England and other European countries today in rectifying the difference. Every year there are more dogs resembling the ideal described in the Standard that are being brought to field trials. May this continue as time goes on and give the Springer his due!

Over the past fifty year period, pedigrees go back to the same dogs and the same strains—Denne, Rivington, Beechgrove, Aqualate, Caistor, Roeland, and Tissington. And fifty years from now, no doubt, all strains in this country will go back to Melilotus, Caulier's, Salilyn, Waiterock, Schwedekrest, Charlyle, Walpride, and the many others building up every year from unions of all the strains in this great era for the breed in North America. May all breeders adhere to the Standard of the times, for it sets the pattern for a type that is beautiful as well as workable—a Springer suitable for just about everything that could be desired in a dog.

Interest is divided, it is true, but how lucky we are to have a breed that can serve a dual purpose. Of course, many Springer fanciers say that the breed is now dual in that we have two types—one for the field and one for the show ring. But it is odd how many field dog owners breed and train dogs which are actually closer in conformation to bench dogs than to some of the field trial regulars. Descriptions of some English field trained champions state that they are beautiful and look the type of the exceedingly well-bred Springer. Pictures of many American field trial champions bear this out, as well. And from the number of kennels that show their dogs in conformation and field

Allan Gilmour.

train them and run them in trials, the trend seems to be going in the right direction.

There are many field trial enthusiasts in the fancy, but there are many more show devotees. In both groups there are hundreds of gun dog addicts who are well satisfied that Springers can do (and are doing) what they have been bred to do for hundreds of years.

And where else can you find a medium-sized dog that hunts close, springs the game to provide top shooting, marks the fall after the shot, and retrieves on command?

Pointers set game but don't always hold pheasants. Setters do the same. Both cover ground so fast and far that the owner can often spend most of his time hunting dogs. Retrievers are good at retrieving, and retrieving ability is an inherent trait for most breeds and so are all forms of water work. This means Retrievers don't have to be taught a great deal. But often their size precludes their being able to hold out all day when hunting on land.

Springers are in a class by themselves in that they were bred to fill a gap in the abilities of other breeds—for a medium-large, tough dog, able to hunt all day in and on all kinds of terrain, and able to do everything needed in order to be a top gun dog. With training locations and conditions what they are in this country today, it is sometimes difficult to train a gun dog. Consequently, a dog bred to do everything you want has an edge on the dog bred to specialize in just one or two of the abilities typical of the good, all-round gun dog.

Frank Wyant, Bill Lane, and John Findorf.

Judges James Stewart and John Blanock, at 1970 Keystone English Springer Spaniel Club Trial.

In the eastern part of the United States there are nine Springer clubs holding field trials. In the mid-section, there are twelve clubs. And on the West Coast, there are ten. Many of these clubs have been organized more than forty years and all endeavor to show the breed in its primary role: that of a rugged dog with skill in hunting, with a great heart for his job, and with great endurance. All Springers are able to participate in training sessions at the clubs. Often a dog shows merit regardless of breeding, as its inherent qualities come to the fore during training sessions.

The first field trial for Springers in the United States was held in New York State in 1924 at the Ferguson estate on Fisher's Island, in an area that was mostly meadowland and was thickly populated with birds. Trials continued here for the next twenty-five years, and Walter Ferguson, who made the site available, did much in those early years to foster Springers and get them established in field trial competition in this country. A bench show was held in conjunction with each of these early trials, and, as a result, much emphasis was placed on the development of dual champions. Two early day duals were made: Tedwyn's Trex, an English import; and Frost, an American-bred Springer. A son of Tedwyn's Trex, Field Trial Ch. Trex of Chancefield, owned, trained, and handled by Francis J. Squires, placed more times in trials than any other dog in America.

Puppy Series, 1970 Bushy Hill Field Trial Association.

Dr. Samuel Milbank handled dogs at these early trials, and his Field Trial Ch. Rivington Countryman placed Second in the 1956 trial. Dr. Milbank continued to handle his own dogs after his eightieth year.

In the thirties and early forties, James Simpson, Jr., was most successful, along with the Armforth Kennels belonging to the late Philip D. Armour, Jr., and Mrs. Armour. Through the years, dogs from Armforth Kennels won four Nationals and many other trials. And Mrs. Armour was the first woman and the only amateur to win the National Open as both owner and handler.

Joseph C. Quirk's Wakes Wager of Greenfair, a field trial champion in England and India, was brought to this country by Mr. Quirk and finished his United States field trial title within his first year of competition. It is interesting to note that despite the fact that this dog was not used much as a sire, his descendants have continued to be among the winners over the years.

Will Sinclair, head gamekeeper for the Fisher's Island Sportsman's Club, Harry Cameron, and Larry Macqueen, along with Martin Hogen and his son-in-law, David G. Lorenz, were among those that helped build the foundation for field trials in the forties. Steve Studnicki, Ruffy Eakin, Chuck Goodall, Luke Medlin, and Elmore Chick made important contributions to the advancement of Springer field trials of the fifties. And in 1960 we have Mrs. Philip D. Armour, Jr., handling her own dog and winning the National Championship Field Trial—the first woman to accomplish this outstanding feat. Another outstanding record was made by Gwibernant Ganol, owned by John Pirie, Jr., and handled by David Lorenz. This Springer won the National Championship Field Trial in 1964 and repeated the win in 1965.

The National Amateur Championship was established in 1962 as a result of efforts led by Charles S. Goodall, Robert McLean, James Dodson, and Richard H. Migel, and augmented by amateur handlers from all over the country. Modeled along the same lines as the National Open Championship Trial, the National Amateur Championship Trial is held annually and is handled by a special committee appointed by the Board of the English Springer Spaniel Field Trial Association. Much interest has been generated by this trial for amateurs. In 1963 and 1964—the first two years the trial was held—twelve Amateur Field Champions resulted. Entries in the National Amateur Championship Trials are owner handled, which is one of the features of this competition.

Judging procedures for field trials were established by the parent club in 1924 and changes have been made as they were needed. Finally, procedures were set up in 1953 by a committee representing all sections of the country, and, as a consequence, the booklet "Conduct and Judging of Spaniel Field Trials" was produced. This publication provides stablized and standardized guidance for the conduct of judges and handlers at trials so that procedure will be in accord at all trials. Copies may be secured by writing the secretary of the parent club, whose name and address are included in current issues of the various dog magazines. The booklet will be of great help to anyone interested in this facet of Springer ownership.

Another publication that will prove helpful to owners interested in field trials is the A.K.C. pamphlet entitled "Registration and Field Trial Rules and Standard Procedures for Pointing Breeds, Dachshunds, Retrievers, Spaniels." Single copies of this pamphlet are available without charge from The American Kennel Club, 51 Madison Avenue, New York, N.Y. 10010. Rules are amended occasionally, so if you have a copy of the regulations, make sure it is current.

Field trial regulations still adhere closely to the rules set down in England nearly one hundred years ago. Most of the changes that have been made are the result of variations in application by judges because conditions in this country are different from those in Great Britain. We have curtailed training and hunting seasons and our shooting grounds are not so readily accessible. And usually we are just too busy to devote the same amount of time to our dogs as is spent on dogs in England and other parts of Europe. Breeding often is more limited in England, so there are fewer English field-bred dogs. The English dogs can be in training almost twelve months of the year, however, and can be run on game birds in natural settings, instead of on planted pigeons on unfamiliar grounds and cover. These are among the reasons that English imports often do very well at our trials.

This phase of Springerdom has much to offer a newcomer to Springers should he prefer the field to the bench. And if the Springer is just a pet, modified field training should result in an improved gun dog. This also applies to an obedience dog, for much of the field training is akin to obedience training and the same schooling is a very integral part of both.

Every gun dog must have some training in the basics of field training. Without knowledge of "come," "hup," and "fetch," the Springer is only a pet dog, and, like a child in the family, has no place in the field where a gun is to be used for hunting game.

"The Cover" at 1970 Keystone English Springer Spaniel Club Field Trial.

Water Series at 1970 Keystone English Springer Spaniel Club Field Trial.

Training the Gun Dog

The first training to be given a gun dog or a field trial dog is yard training, for it tends to establish a rapport between owner and dog—which is primarily what you want to accomplish, although the pleasure of having a field-trained dog can never be overrated. The basic commands the dog will learn in yard training are the "come," the "hup," and the "fetch."

You must teach the dog to come to you instantly—regardless of what he might be doing and under all conditions. You must teach the dog to "hup" (to sit) and to stay in the sitting position until you give him further instructions. And you must teach the dog to "fetch" when (and only when) you command him to do so. Unless he learns these three lessons and learns them well, he will not be under your control in the field and will be of little value to you as a gun dog—and of virtually no value whatsoever in field competition.

Although the dog must have a certain amount of field experience before he really learns control, yard training is the foundation upon which control is taught, and it is essential that the dog learn each step thoroughly before going on to more advanced work.

Prior to the time you start yard training, it is important that the puppy comprehend a few simple commands. For instance, he should understand the meaning of the word "no," and he should associate his name with himself. In addition, he should be housebroken. Information on training the dog along these lines is given in the chapter beginning on page 97.

Before yard training is undertaken, the dog should be fitted with a chain link collar (see page 101) and should become accustomed to wearing it. In addition, he should learn to walk at heel (as described on page 102), first on a loose lead and later without the lead.

It is essential, too, that the Springer be sufficiently mature before training is begun—that the playful, puppy stage be over. Most important of all, it is essential that a feeling of rapport between dog and handler be developed before training is begun. If the handler has been responsible for the feeding, grooming, and general care of the dog for a matter of weeks, has taken him for short walks, and has romped with him and taught him basic "house" manners, dog and handler will

share the feelings of mutual love and respect that are essential before training can be undertaken successfully.

It is also essential that the handler understand what is to be expected of the Springer in the field before he starts training the dog. Although it may be an over-simplified version of a somewhat complex procedure, the following paragraph describes the Springer's activities in the field.

The well-trained Springer in the field is under control at all times. He walks at his handler's side without forging ahead, whether he is on lead or off. He "hups" (sits) immediately when his handler gives the command and remains in position until his handler gives him further instructions. When his handler gives the command, he begins immediately and eagerly to hunt in the direction the handler indicates by hand signal. He then quarters back and forth in front of his handler—that is, he moves back and forth across the field, crossing in front of the handler at a distance of from five to ten yards and moving out to either side of him at a distance of perhaps thirty yards. When he scents game, he shows great animation and moves in on the bird and causes it to take flight. When the bird is airborne, the dog "hups" and remains in the "hup" position until the bird is dropped. He keeps his eyes on the location at which the bird falls until his handler gives the command to retrieve. He then moves eagerly to the area where the bird fell and searches until he locates it. He seizes the bird firmly but with a soft mouth and returns rapidly to his handler. He "hups" at the handler's feet and offers the bird to him until the handler commands "give," when he releases the bird. He then remains in the "hup" position until his handler provides further instructions.

In training the dog, it is important to remember two things: first, schedule the daily training session before feeding the dog, and make a game of it so both you and he enjoy it; second, don't overdo the training session. To maintain the rapport between you and the dog with no evidence of bad humor or ill temper, you must never continue the session for too long a period of time.

Training sessions should be conducted in a quiet place, away from such distractions as might be created by traffic, people, other dogs, or pets. For the first few lessons, you may wish to work with your Springer indoors—particularly if the weather is bad. But before long you should be working with him out-of-doors in a secluded area. Later, you should take him to fields and woods where he will come in contact with rabbits, squirrels, and birds.

Making yourself the "center of interest" to your pupil is the most

important aspect of all training, says Talbot Radcliff in *Spaniels for Sport*. I agree, and I think you will, too, after you have given the subject a bit of thought. Faults in a dog's response to commands are usually attributable to the trainer. Dogs learn by repetition, so be consistent—and fair—at all times. And make sure you have the dog's attention before you give a command.

To train the dog to "come," attach a forty or fifty foot rope line to his collar. Walk a short distance away (the distance will depend to some extent upon the size of your training area), and command him to "come." Speak in a firm, clear voice. If the dog hesitates while coming, use the rope to start him at once—or to drag him, if necessary.

Whenever you give your dog commands, speak in a firm, distinct voice, and make sure that the dog understands each command. Dogs learn the meaning of hand signals quite readily, so use an appropriate hand signal along with the verbal commands during yard training. The dog will then learn to respond to hand signals in the field whether he hears the command or not.

In the beginning, limit your training session to a period of no more than four or five minutes, and limit the number of training sessions to two a day. Continue the training sessions until the dog comes on command without hesitation. Four or five lessons should perfect the dog's response to the "come" command.

After he has learned to "come," the next command the dog is to be taught is the "hup," a contraction of "hie up"—a command to sit. (The "hup" is also used by most handlers to command the dog to stay until he is given further instructions, although some handlers prefer to use the command "stay" for this purpose.)

To teach the dog to "hup," take him on a short lead to the training area, and with the dog at heel, stop, give the command "Hup," place your left hand on the dog's rear and your right hand under his chin. Repeating the command "Hup," press down with your left hand and lift his chin with the right, forcing him to sit. You will note that the "hup" is taught in the same basic manner as is the "sit," the procedure for which is described on page 102.

Here, again, lessons should be limited to a period of four or five minutes only, and training sessions should be limited to no more than two a day. The training sessions can be gradually increased in length as the dog grows older, but sessions should still be limited to two a day.

During training sessions, do not concentrate on the "hup" com-

Ch. Beryltown Virginian of Pequa, Best in Sweepstakes, and Ch. Beryltown Lively Victoria, Best of Opposite Sex, at EESSC Specialty Show, 1966. Both are by Ch. Charlyle's Fair Warning ex Ch. Beryltown Lively Rocket.

mand alone, but also include practice of the "come" exercise the dog has already learned. Also, throughout the day, whenever the occasion arises, use the commands "come" and "hup" to keep your dog under control.

When the dog performs well, it is most important that you reward him by praising and petting. Let him know that you are highly pleased with his response to your commands.

Once the dog has mastered the "come" and the "hup" (sit) commands, teach him to remain in the "hup" position until you give him further instructions. To do this, you will need to use the rope line and a stake with a screw eye inserted at the top.

When you and your dog arrive at the training area, command him to "hup" and insert the stake in the ground near him. Then run the line through the screw eye and fasten one end of the line securely to the dog's chain link collar. Grasping the other end of the line, give the command "Hup," and slowly back away, meanwhile repeating the "hup" command. Should the dog attempt to follow you, simply hold the line taut and he will be unable to do so. When you are ready to have the dog move, give the "come" command, releasing your grip on the rope so that the dog can move toward you. Just before the dog reaches you, give the "hup" command and stop the dog with the rope.

The above procedures teach the two commands that are used most. If you make a game of teaching him, your dog will soon become almost automatic in responding to either of the commands. All success later depends on how well he learns and obeys these first two commands.

When your dog "hups" on command and "comes" on command and then "hups" when he reaches you, he is well on his way to becoming an accomplished field or gun dog. The next step, of course, is the "fetch"—teaching your dog to retrieve. Short lessons on retrieving should be begun before the dog is a year old, but this portion of the dog's training is so important that I will discuss it by itself in the next chapter.

If you have shot over good gun dogs, you will not experience much difficulty in working with your dog. You know what you want. But to a novice with his first gun or field dog, this may seem most complicated. It can be just the opposite, however, if you think of it as fun and concentrate on the rapport it generates between you and your dog.

Yes, "come," "hup," and "fetch" cover a lot of territory. There are many side issues connected with the three commands, and a dog will do what he is trained to do. But he will not perform with the style and

verve that constitute his inbred potential if training is overdone. So keep it fun, and you will have fun as well, for the Springer is the world's greatest all-purpose dog: house dog, hunting companion, four-legged pal, and friend.

In an earlier chapter in this book I told you of my first experience in hunting with a good gun dog—an overgrown Cocker-bred dog that was all liver and could pass, today, as a Springer. He was never trained beyond "come," "hup," and "fetch," but he had the bloodlines and the intestinal fortitude from centuries of breeding from fine ancestors that equipped him to become an exceptional gun dog. Chances are that he was a descendant of such dogs as were listed simply as Spaniels, but he provided me with a great insight into the potential of the English Springer Spaniel.

Another experience which afforded me great insight into Springer character and potential occurred about forty years ago when I first lived in Pennsylvania. A friend asked me to go along to Newcastle, Pennsylvania, to go pheasant hunting. I arrived at his home about 5:00 a.m., and while we were eating breakfast he asked if I was willing to have another hunter go along. The other hunter, it seemed, was a good friend of my friend, and, besides, he had a good dog. Naturally, I agreed, and so we drove over to pick up the hunter and his dog. Out they came—a large, gray-haired man and a gorgeous, bouncing, liver and white dog, which he told us was an English Springer Spaniel and belonged to his son. The son, he said, lived in a ten-story apartment house and the dog had never been in a field before. He did say, however, that he and his son had shot over the dog the day his son brought him to Newcastle and that the dog wasn't gunshy.

We arrived at the farm where we were to hunt, unloaded our gear, and started to hunt—joined by the owner of the farm. And what a day! We shot pheasants, quail, and a couple of grouse, all worked to perfection by that dog. He hunted, quartered, found game for four guns, and retrieved (including a half-mile downhill retrieve), and he couldn't have been better if he'd been trained by a professional.

Another time I took an old pensioner, "Spot," my first Springer, out back of the kennels on the last day of the season. He had been kenneled all season because of his age, blindness, and deafness, and had been acting as though he felt very neglected. So I got a gun and we took off in the direction of a small swamp about a hundred yards from the kennel—a favorite retreat for both birds and deer. Sure enough, out went a cock. Spot heard it for it went right over his head as he poked his nose in a blackberry tangle. The bird sailed down to

Ch. Kaintuck Pixie, Best of Opposite Sex at the 1968 Westminster Kennel Club Show.

the edge of the woods and Spot started down, too—with his nose in the air. I sat down on a log and watched him bang into trees and everything else between that bird and himself. After a while I heard the bird cackle again, and he took off coming back toward me. I shot and the bird dropped into the very center of the blackberry tangle. I sat down again, blew the whistle once, and waited. A few moments later, poor Spot stumbled into view, but I stayed where I was on the log and watched in amazement as he slowly made his way into the berry patch, still scenting. He was scratched by the blackberry thorns as he tried to find a way to that bird, and finally he went down on his belly and slid under the bushes. He went all the way in and picked up that bird. He came out with its wings in his mouth and the body across his muzzle. He stood there, in the late afternoon sun, trying to locate me. Evidently the scent of the dead bird overpowered my scent, since I was about twenty feet away. So I rose and slowly made my way to him. He gave me the bird and I stuffed it into my coat, gave him a pat, and went back to the log where I could sit down, put my arm around him, and cry a little, for I knew that was his last bird after his many years of hunting with me.

This is another example of the effectiveness of the "come," "hup," and "fetch" training, for that was the only training Spot had ever had. But he had been broken to shot considerably, and he had been "humanized" in his early association with me.

Judges: Colonel Ray Costabile and Bus Flick.

Back row: Dean Bedford, William Lane, C. Wingate. Front row: Cliff Wallace, L. MacQueen, and Art Mayer.

"Guns": Jim Stewart, Russ Wilson, Joel Lovell, Frank Wyant, and Paul Thompson.

Back row: Ron Madecy, John Findorf, and Frank Wyant. Front row: Allan Gilmour, Larry MacQueen, and Elmore Chick.

Retrieving

It has been said that "A natural retrieve is a gem beyond price," and that is plain, understated truth. How else can you save game and get everything (or nearly everything) you shoot, thus preventing needless slaughter and waste.

In a Springer, the ability to retrieve is an inherent trait. With proper training and sufficient practice, this natural ability can be polished to the point of perfection. And this is the purpose of training your dog, for accuracy in locating birds is highly desirable, and excellent retrieving is one of the great trademarks of a Springer.

Before he is old enough to start training, get your Springer interested in picking up a knotted handkerchief or other soft object which he can see easily when you throw it. When he sees you throw the object, the Springer will, as a rule, race after it, pick it up, and return to offer it to you. When he brings the object, do not snatch it from him or engage in a tug of war. Doing either will tend to develop a "hard mouth"—the habit of biting down hard on the object—and later on the bird.

Also, if you take your dog as a pup into the field to acquaint him with all the obstacles there, to get a sniff of feathers or even of fur, he will learn faster when he reaches training age.

The best time to start short, five-minute lessons on retrieving is shortly before your dog is a year old. When you tossed the knotted handkerchief to the puppy, he made an instant retrieve or not according to his mood. But now that he is old enough to be trained and you are helping him to fulfill his destiny, he must respond with alacrity. When it comes to the training sessions themselves, you must never get frazzled, you must never throw intelligence aside, you must never allow your temper to get thin. You must control yourself first if you are to control the dog.

In training the dog to retrieve—just as in teaching the "come" and the "hup"—training sessions must be interspersed with periods of fun, with periodic recesses, and with plenty of rewards in the form of petting and praise when the dog performs well. If it is necessary to punish him, hold onto your temper and be just in your chastisement.

Get a dummy—a rolled-up newspaper, a corn cob, a small boat bumper, or whatever. The training collar, the strong rope line (pre-

ferably a line of small diameter of the clothesline type), a whistle, and a blank cartridge pistol constitute the other equipment required.

First of all, you should take your dog to the training area for several sessions of review of the "come" and the "hup" commands, but now you will substitute a series of short, sharp blasts on the whistle for the "come" command. With the training rope attached to the dog's collar, blow a series of sharp chirping blasts on the whistle, and give a quick tug on the line. Usually, the dog makes the transition from the verbal commands to the whistle with little difficulty, but if the dog hesitates for any length of time, tug harder, and he'll get the message.

The "hup" command is so important that we'll go over it again. With the dog on your left in the "heel" position, place your left hand on the dog's rear and your right hand under his chin. Give the command, press down with your left hand and lift his chin with the right, forcing him to sit. Most handlers use one sharp blast on the whistle for "hup," a series of short notes for the "come" (as described above), and two sharp blasts close together to turn or change direction.

Make the dog stay on the "hup" until you want him to move again. When he has learned this lesson, move away, walk around him, and make him continue to "hup," or stay. Change tactics as you do this—walking away, calling to him, making him "hup" on both verbal and whistle commands—all to enable you to handle him and to keep him under control at all times.

The "come" and the "hup" are two of the most important commands he will ever learn, so it is essential that he learn them well.

And now to the "fetch," the final facet of the "ABC's" of field training. Now it is no game but something important.

With the dog in the "hup" position, hold the collar and gently open his mouth. Place the dummy in the dog's mouth and make him hold it until you give the command "Give." (As with earlier practice with the knotted handkerchief, it is important that you refrain from snatching the dummy from him or engaging in a tug of war.) Keep practicing until he actually helps by taking the dummy without pressure and relinquishes it as soon as you give the command. As a variation, make him hold the dummy while you walk away. (Each time he performs as directed, praise him and pet him.) Command "Fetch," and warn him to hold the dummy. Practice until he will walk around with something in his mouth and give it to you on command. And after a week or two, substitute larger dummies.

Don't overwork the dog on the retrieves. Make a game of his carrying things proudly and eagerly. Limit each training session to fifteen minutes or less, making sure the dog does not become overtired, but schedule one or two sessions each day. And don't forget to praise him and pet him when he responds well.

Once the dog has mastered this step, start having him pick up the dummy from the ground. After a few days' practice on this procedure, throw the dummy a few feet away and command him to "fetch" it to you. Never force him to get it more than once or twice without a recess. Be sure that throwing out the dummy and retrieving it is fun for him and part of a game. Give him a reward in the form of petting and praise when he does his part. As he grows more proficient, begin to throw the dummy where he will need to use his nose to find it.

When he has learned to retrieve the dummy under all these varying circumstances, it is time to use the feathered wing so that he will become accustomed to a mouthful of feathers. When he takes the wing readily, use a live pigeon with its wings locked and its feet taped. Once he has learned to retrieve the pigeon for you, dizzy a pigeon, throw it out, and shoot it for retrieving practice. If an older dog is available, shoot the pigeon and let the older dog retrieve it while the younger one watches. Do this several times and then throw out a bird, shoot it, and let the pup retrieve it. If he doesn't bring the dead pigeon to you, force him to go out and pick it up.

Remember this isn't accomplished all in one day or one session. It must be undertaken slowly and sensibly so as not to become tiresome either to you or to the youngster.

Noise conditioning is an important factor in developing a reliable field dog that is not gunshy. Before you start shooting pigeons for the dog to retrieve, it is essential that you gradually condition him to the sound of the gun. An excellent way to begin the conditioning is to fire a cap pistol from a short distance away as you approach your dog with his food. Then he will associate the sound with the pleasure of eating. Once he has become accustomed to the cap pistol and shows no signs of nervousness when he hears the report, you should expose him to other noises under pleasurable circumstances. For instance, take the puppy to the field and permit him to chase squirrels or rabbits or simply to run about. Then, while he is intent on what he is doing, fire .22 blanks at a little distance from him. If he exhibits no nervousness to the sound of the .22 blank, gradually condition him to the sound of the .410 gauge. But here, too, begin the conditioning when the dog is some distance away and is intent on chasing game or

running about the field. The need for care and caution in the use of the gun cannot be stressed too strongly. You must be careful never to shoot directly over the head of the dog or another person, for the sound of the shot at close range can damage the hearing irreparably.

Conditioning the dog to noise gradually is of the utmost importance. A dog that develops gunshyness can rarely be cured, and months of re-education are usually required if a cure is to be effected.

Although I have never tried this method, I have been told that the best way to overcome gunshyness is to take the dog out into a lake and let him swim—then shoot and make sure he sees you shooting, so he will know what is causing the noise. Because the dog is swimming, he won't be able to run off and hide someplace. And seeing how the noise is caused should help him overcome his fear.

As your dog becomes proficient in the field, he must be steady to flush and shot. He must not charge out when he flushes the bird

Ch. Beryltown Lively Chatter, CDX.

but must stay down until you give the command to move, for you don't want him in the way of a shot. Watch your dog when you shoot and make him stay in the "hup" position so that he doesn't interfere with your shot or chase the bird into the next county if you miss it when you shoot.

To teach the dog to be steady, stand him in front of you and give the "hup" command. Toss the feathered dummy over your shoulder and repeat the "hup" command. If the dog attempts to move, grab his collar and enforce the command as you again repeat the "hup." If the dog continues to require restraint, scold him in a stern voice. It may be necessary to repeat the lesson several times, but the dog should never be permitted to retrieve until his handler gives the command to "fetch," either verbally or with the whistle. Here, again, it is important to remember to praise the dog and to pet him when he performs well.

Teach your dog to "go out" and then use the whistle and/or hand signals to move him around in the field—perhaps into a briar patch, or to look for an unmarked bird. And remember, only actual work and plenty of it can make a field dog.

In training the dog to quarter, attract his attention with the whistle and then use hand signals to indicate that he is to turn and move in the opposite direction. It will be much easier to train the dog to quarter if you habitually follow a zigzag pattern when you take the dog through fields during early lessons and always work into the wind. It is essential that the dog learn to quarter the ground properly so that he will not range so far ahead of you that the game he flushes is beyond gunshot. Preferably, the game should be within thirty yards of the hunter when it is flushed.

Proper working of the cover requires experience on the part of the dog. Make sure there is game, and plenty of it, in the field where you start this part of his education so that he gets plenty of exercise plus plenty of experience and still has fun.

Take your training cord with you and use it if you run into a problem and have to review the training routines. Don't hurry this phase of field work, for all errors are magnified if they occur too often. They must be stopped before they become habits.

It is important to remember not to baby your dog. When you start actual training, make him follow you regardless of fences, ditches, briars, water, or anything else that might distress him or make him want help. When you take him to the field, let your dog do the hunting. Don't coddle him. Let him get used to taking his bumps, and once his puppy days are over and he is a working member of the house-

hold, let him work out his own problems. Dogs should hunt naturally, and in field trial work, those that do so are given credit over those that require continued voice or whistle commands.

However, a well-trained field dog should keep track of his handler, so make sure that he always works with you as a part of a team. Never let him run off where you can't see him. If he shows a tendency to wander too far away, either call him or whistle him in. This is where the "come" command is most important. It is essential that you keep control over your dog at all times, but handle him with as few commands as possible.

After your dog has become proficient at retrieving on land, start him on water work. If possible, start him with an older dog that has had experience with retrieving from water. In any event, the first time you take him to the lake or pond, you should wear waders, for it will probably be necessary for you to enter the water too.

First of all, allow the dog to investigate the area for several minutes. Then call him and walk out a few feet into the water. The dog most likely will follow. Probably he will frisk about. Perhaps he will dash back to shore and then back into the water as he becomes accustomed to this new experience. If he attempts to swim, encourage him to continue. If he doesn't make any effort to swim, you may have to walk out farther so that he will do so. Several trips to the water may be necessary before the dog acquires confidence in this new medium, but if you are patient and encourage him sufficiently, the dog will be fully acclimated before long. Once the young dog is at home in the water, have the older dog make several retrieves. Then have the younger one "hup" and fetch" on his own.

When the commands "come," "hup," and "fetch" (given both verbally and by whistle) are thoroughly mastered on both land and water, you have a dog ready for advanced field training and a gun dog ready to go. If his training has been fun, he won't want to miss a minute of being out with you in the big, wide world.

And from there on in, you can go hunting or you can go on and field train your dog. Either way, you will have a good dog trained in the basic duties and principles that make him a very fine hunting companion, a dog capable of doing a good day's work with you in the field and fulfilling the aims of breeders over the past several centuries whose purpose was to produce a dog capable of doing everything required on land and water—to be a companion to his owner and give him love and devotion with every living breath, and to be known to the world as *your Springer Spaniel.*